T0398728

Integral Innovation

Technology plays a critical role in transforming societies and economies through enhancing efficiency, connectivity and access to resources and services. The challenge remains how to harness technologies to achieve sustainable development without causing harm to human and natural capitals.

Professor Odeh Rashed Al-Jayyousi argues that science, technology and innovation (STI) are underpinned by social choices and, hence, a transition to a sustainable green economy is defined by individuals' and institutions' decisions on how to use and apply these STI developments. It is, therefore, important to examine closely the ways in which social institutions and processes in the "integral worlds" (the different perspectives of reality) shape the priorities of technologies and the conditions under which their potential benefits can be reaped. He states that in order for technological innovation to provide a guarantee of sustainable economic development, it is necessary that a transfer of technology to developing countries becomes a basic principle of national development policies, and that they, in turn, are open to adopting an explicit long-term application of technological innovation.

Integral Innovation: New Worldviews presents a conceptual framework for the evolution of technology and innovation from a historical and cultural perspective. It provides an analysis of the role of innovation and technology in sustainable development and introduces a number of international case studies, which shed light on the social learning processes for knowledge co-creation and innovation culture. It is essential reading for those interested in innovation and technology management.

Odeh Rashed Al-Jayyousi has been Professor and Head of Innovation and Technology Management at Arabian Gulf University in Bahrain since September 2015. He was the Vice President for Science and Research at the Royal Scientific Society in Jordan during the period of 2011–2013. He was the Regional Director for the Middle East regional office of IUCN – International Union for Conservation of

Nature (headquartered in Switzerland) – throughout 2004–2011. Previously, he was Dean of Scientific Research and a university professor in Water Resources and Environment during the period of 1994–2004. He was an academic director for the MSc Programme in Transformational Management in the UK. His research interests include water and environmental policy, sustainable development, innovation management, technology foresight, green technology and smart cities. He has published several books including *Islam and Sustainable Development* (2012) and a book on renewable energy and knowledge sharing in the Arab world (2015). He was granted an award for Scientists and Social Initiatives in 2014.

Transformation and Innovation
Series editors: Ronnie Lessem and Alexander Schieffer

This series on enterprise transformation and social innovation comprises a range of books informing practitioners, consultants, organization developers, development agents and academics how businesses and other organizations, as well as the discipline of economics itself, can and will have to be transformed. The series prepares the ground for viable twenty-first-century enterprises and a sustainable macroeconomic system. A new kind of R&D, involving social, as well as technological innovation, needs to be supported by integrated and participative action research in the social sciences. Focusing on new, emerging kinds of public, social and sustainable entrepreneurship originating from all corners of the world and from different cultures, books in this series will help those operating at the interface between enterprise and society to mediate between the two and will help schools teaching management and economics to re-engage with their founding principles.

For a full list of titles in this series, please visit www.routledge.com/business/series/TANDI

Integral Ubuntu Leadership
Passmore Musungwa Matupire

Islam and Sustainable Development
New Worldviews
Odeh Rashed Al-Jayyousi

Integral Community Enterprise in Africa
Communitalism as an Alternative to Capitalism
Anselm Adodo

Integral Innovation
New Worldviews
Odeh Rashed Al-Jayyousi

Integral Innovation

New Worldviews

ODEH RASHED AL-JAYYOUSI

Routledge
Taylor & Francis Group

LONDON AND NEW YORK

First published 2017
by Routledge
2 Park Square, Milton Park, Abingdon, Oxon OX14 4RN

and by Routledge
711 Third Avenue, New York, NY 10017

Routledge is an imprint of the Taylor & Francis Group, an informa business

British Library Cataloguing in Publication Data
A catalogue record for this book is available from the British Library

Library of Congress Cataloging in Publication Data
Names: Al-Jayyousi, Odeh, author.
Title: Integral innovation : new worldviews / Odeh Al-Jayyousi.
Description: New York : Routledge, 2017. | Includes index.
Identifiers: LCCN 2016054609 | ISBN 9781472481061 (hardback) | ISBN 9781315588957 (ebook)
Subjects: LCSH: Technological innovations.
Classification: LCC HC79.T4 A415 2017 | DDC 338/.064--dc23
LC record available at https://lccn.loc.gov/2016054609

ISBN: 978-1-4724-8106-1 (hbk)
ISBN: 978-1-315-58895-7 (ebk)

Typeset in Palatino
by Saxon Graphics Ltd, Derby

To my parents who are the *spring for innovation.*

To my brothers Majid, Khalil, Khaldoun and Ahmad who are *champions in innovation.*

To my sisters Wedad, Hedaya and Jamileh who are the *oases of inspiration.*

To my wife Saheer Jallad who is the *ecosystem for innovation.*

To my children Muath, Noor, Leena and Omar who are the *drivers of innovation.*

To Jayousi pioneer women who embraced education as a mission: Bakreyeh, Nada, Salma, Fatima, Ghada and Hayat who are *models of excellence in innovation.*

To all refugees of the world who are the *catalysts of innovation.*

Contents

Figures

Tables

Preface

This book is an extension of my book *Islam and Sustainable Development: New Worldviews* which was first published in 2012. Sustainable innovation (*ijtihad*) is underpinned by an enlightened understanding and interpretation of culture, economy and society to address the current global issues and to seek a common articulation which is founded on reconciliation, reconstruction, human emancipation, dignity and freedom.

In this book, *Integral Innovation*, I attempt to transcend the boundaries of markets and governments to ecology, society and culture. The innovation journey in this book is framed by the "innovation-sustainability nexus". It is a purposeful attempt at reconstruction of an innovative Individual, Community, Organization and Nation (ICON), an essential ingredient and enabler for renewal and enlightenment.

One of the key questions that I attempt to explore is how nations acquire or lose their innovative capacity and what the conditions and enablers are for sustaining a culture of innovation in both organizations and nations. The innovation-sustainability nexus underpins the journey of innovation management in the domains of ideas, individuals, and organizations. Reflecting on the cycles of history and the rise and fall of civilizations, we realize that innovation emerges after a state of de-construction or an unsteady state. Hence, I argue that refugees play a vital role in innovation through swimming upstream. Paradoxically, the Islamic civilization, like the Roman Empire, was faced with a set of challenges that hindered the sustainability of innovation and the culture of open innovation and societal reflection. Although the Islamic civilization contributed to enlightenment and scientific discoveries in the Golden Age, the ecosystem, culture and social DNA of innovation is not deeply rooted in the local context in the twenty-first century.

Integral innovation is a purposeful effort to navigate through different types, forms and phases of innovation (social, ecological, institutional, technological and economic) to deepen our understanding of the DNA of social change, technical progress and sustainability. The interface between culture and innovation needs to be explored to unlock the human potential and value the contributions of all cultures and nations in the journey for a sustainable future. In a nutshell, the prosperity of humankind is underpinned by our ability to embrace openness and celebrate diversity through cross-fertilization and fusion of innovative ideas from all cultures.

While *civilization educates, culture enlightens* and hence we need to seek enlightenment for inducing innovation that is lodged in culture and ecology. Integral innovation implies the ability of seeing systems, networks and webs of life. The basic notion of unity (*tawheed*) in the Islamic worldview has immense implications to see "systems" and unity in sciences (natural and social), unity in art and science, unity in human origin and destiny, and unity in all cultures. This cosmic, human and ecological unity is a clear manifestation of the oneness of this integral innovation. Hence, human imagination and the holistic notions of innovation are inspired by the cosmos, ecology, culture and human history.

Integral innovation is simply about the "internet of ideas" and the web of cultures that shape science and technology to develop a sustainable future for humanity. The history of technological innovation is simply the narrative of humankind pursuing a good, safe, efficient and comfortable life. I intend to look at the hidden connections and cycles in ecology, history and business to shed light on a possible newly emerging paradigm of integral innovation. In a market economy that views the value of the "world of things", we end up losing sight of the value of the "world of ideas". Economics has framed the current development model, but it is of crucial significance that development thinking should be reformed by ecology and culture.

After 2011, or what was called the "Arab Spring" which resulted in a state of instability and destruction in the Middle East and North Africa (MENA) region, it has become imperative to rethink and revisit the foundations of Science, Technology, and Innovation (STI) as a driver for prosperity and development. This implies the imperative to harness the essence of innovation in all domains of life to enable individuals, organizations and societies to embody new worldviews for a sustainable human civilization based on adaptation, co-existence, resilience, reconciliation, tolerance, open and collective innovation, and societal renewal. STI for sustainable development was viewed as a driving force and an overarching theme for the UN Post 2015 Agenda; however, innovative nations, organizations and individuals are key ingredients for transforming this vision to into reality. The MENA region should be mindful of the role of STI in founding and nurturing sustainable organizations, cities, societies and nations through good governance, partnerships, civic intelligence and ethics.

Cities and communities are viewed as a living laboratory for innovation since they reflect the level of aligning and harnessing of the financial capital with social, natural, manufactured and intellectual capitals. Our human collective efforts will be fruitful in integral innovation when we are able to revive and reconstruct the smart Arab cities in the Gulf Cooperation Council countries and in turbulent states like Yemen, Syria, Libya, Iraq, Palestine and Sudan. The ability to organize the built environment in the public and private institutions, infrastructure, services and STI should be part of a transformative vision to move beyond the state of *creative destruction* to one of *innovative reconstruction*. The refugees should be viewed as an opportunity, new ingredient and driving force for socio-eco-innovation, as they always used to be in Europe and the USA, rather than a threat or risk. The influx of refugees in all parts of the world represents a state of "bounded instability" to introduce new insights for integral innovation, global governance, business models, new consciousness and leadership.

The historical initiatives in the nineteenth century for reform and renewal in the MENA region emphasized both cultural and technological innovations. The future of the MENA region will be underpinned by the ability to reform a new discourse for an "innovative culture" along with institutional and technological infrastructure and an ecosystem for STI. The innovation-sustainability nexus implies the need to define key conditions related to renewal and innovation to form an identity and a sense of unity within global diversity and to revitalize a renewed Islamic discourse that deepens and contextualizes the notion of a "median community" (*ummah wassat*) and hence celebrates co-existence, cultural diversity and integral innovation.

An integral innovation requires the embodiment of an eco-cosmic ethos and a new educational system that balances *spiritual, ecological and cultural dimensions* including art, local knowledge and heritage. It also implies accepting differences as a source of enrichment, resilience and vitality. On the other hand, integral innovation is fuelled by both ecological and cultural diversity to frame and define global and regional commons to achieve public interest and collective rational actions. In a globalized world that faces potential risks due to poverty, disease, unemployment, climate change, energy security and refugees, it is insightful to harness and unlock this human capital for innovative forces that can transform scarcity to abundance and challenges and risks to opportunities.

An enabler and a cornerstone for cultural renewal is transformative education that focuses on design thinking. The innovative education system is the bedrock for socio-technological transformation. However, the history of civilizations in terms of STI is documented in a selective and cross-sectional fashion with an absence of dialogue about the historical legacy of Islamic civilization in Western formal education. Hence, it is imperative to co-create proper platforms that nurture diversity and celebrate the collective cross-cultural contributions in human civilization.

In the twenty-first century, there is still a need for an innovative reading of local knowledge, culture and heritage in light of the globalized market economy, social relativism and commodification of cultures. Social, cultural, and open and user innovation can offer new possibilities for addressing poverty, governance, human health, resource depletion and climate change.

I see innovation in a multi-dimensional space and time that encompasses all human endeavours for the pursuit of a good, sustainable and resilient life. In other words, innovation is a collective societal worldview that is informed and fuelled by leadership, governance and vision. This vision is embedded in philosophy and culture which is a form of positive and renewable energy available for transforming ICON innovation.

However, in many developing countries there is a disconnect between the four pillars of innovation (ICON) and there is also another disconnect at the core as manifested in dislocation of culture and ecology from technical and economic innovation due to the linking of modernization with Westernization during the colonial era. These two systemic and structural barriers currently limit the propensity to innovate at all levels.

To conclude, the Western search for reasoning and discovery in science and technology resulted in a separation of science and religion, and state and religion. However, this dichotomy does not, and should not, exist in the Islamic worldview, since the trajectory of science and technology progress did not suffer from the Western syndrome of separation in the MENA region; instead it is about *tawheed*. This linkage or correlation between innovation and cultural values needs to be explored and examined further to dispel the hypothesis that religious beliefs can pose constraints on human innovative capacity. Integral innovation in the Islamic worldview resonates with notions of unity, coherence and value creation.

Acknowledgements

I wish to thank many who contributed to make this book see light. Mohamad Saeed Abdeen, CEO of Industrial Abdeen, Jordan; Dr. Rana Dajani, university professor at Hashemite University, Jordan and Head of Change-NGO; and Prof. Waleed Zubari, Head of the Water Team at Arabian Gulf University, Bahrain for the provision of case studies. In addition, thanks are due to Dr. Afaf Buqawa, Ahmad Al-Rifai, Muath Jayousi and Maheen Al-Bastaki for the technical support and production of graphics. Also, I would like to extend my sincere thanks to Prof. Ahmed Kholei and Prof. Medani Bendari for their comments on the manuscript.

1

Setting the scene: integral innovation

Innovation is simply about seeing the missing links and acting on connecting them; it is about harnessing the web of ideas to add value and achieve competitive advantage for nations, communities, organizations, and individuals.

(The author)

We are born as innovative individuals but this natural talent is likely to be constrained by existing organizational structures and lack of a proper national system for innovation.

(The author)

1.1 Overview

Innovation is underpinned by culture and ecology which is beyond economics and business models. Getting inspiration from ecology and people is a driving force that illuminates my professional career. Social, ecological and open innovation are crucial for contributing to making a sense of meaning, purpose and value for human existence. Innovation is about transcending science to art and adding value to the community, city and nation. This book aims to present a holistic view for innovation with a focus on ecology and society. It is simply about integral innovation that includes Individual, Community (or city), Organizational and National (ICON) innovation as the domain of action and reflection. In terms of theory and practice, I looked at another four dimensions: Cultural (or social), Ecological, Technological and Economic (CETE) innovation. This book intends to shed light on the above eight dimensions with a number of case studies to show relevance, convergence and the possibility for fusion of ideas.

CHAPTER OBJECTIVES

The main objectives of this chapter are to:

- Shed light on the history and philosophy of science and technology;

- Frame science, technology and innovation (STI) discourse in the developing world;

- Seek inspiration from culture and local knowledge for new models of social and eco-innovations;

- Explore the role of innovation in social renewal and transformation;

- Investigate the key features and conditions for innovative nations, organizations and individuals.

1.2 Introduction: reflections and context

My visit to Hawar Island in Bahrain with graduate students from Arabian Gulf University in 2016 was a source of inspiration for open and eco-innovation which are the core of transformative and integral innovation. Students of technology management and innovation, and environmental science were exploring the value of oysters, seagrass and the process of pearl formation. The reflections and inspirations from graduate students were beyond the limited domain of innovation as confined to the innovation of a product, process or paradigm; it was simply about integral innovation.

What is the most important element for life and the sustainability of a forest or marine life? I raised this question to students of innovation and technology management, ecology, knowledge management, ecology of organizations and leadership to seek some insights on the hidden connections in ecology. The diverse and multiple answers that I compiled were focused on the parts (roots, leaves, oxygen or soil) not on the whole (the ecosystem). Innovation is simply about the whole and systems that connect the parts to make new meaning and value. It is not about the oxygen, or the sun or the leaves of the tree, but rather it is about the photosynthesis and interaction of elements to form new compounds. It is not about the water or fish, but about the marine ecosystem that is linked to the universe and human sustainability. This book is about the integration, fusion and fission of ideas co-creating a new model of innovation.

In my personal journey, I have had the chance to travel around the world and reflect on the various dimensions of innovation: from history to culture, to economy and ecology, to organization and local communities, and to cities and nations. Technical and organizational innovations are inseparable; there are seamless connections between social and cultural innovation on one hand, and ecological, technological and economic/business innovation on the other. This book is simply about shedding light on the unity (*tawheed*) and interconnection of these forms of innovation; ideas and how we experience space, time and people shaping our human memory. Innovation is the confluence and fusion between art and science; industry, society and ecology. Managing ideas, attention and linkages between parts and the whole together reinforces innovations at the ICON levels.

My impressions of and reflections on pearl formation in Bahrain, the Islamic museum in Doha, the forests in Costa Rica, the water cave in Lebanon, the Kruger Park in South Africa, the cactus in Mexico, Islamic calligraphy in Malaysia and Gurnee Island in Senegal, among others, had instilled in me new perspectives on innovations from society and ecology. It widened the scope of innovation to include enlightenment, emancipation, empowerment and sustainability. I believe that innovations encompass all dimensions of life, from philosophy, culture, education, history, economics and the environment. It is not fair to limit innovation to only market and commodities as it deprives the world of ideas, images and notions of the value of creation.

This book is an extension of my book *Islam and Sustainable Development: New Worldviews*, which was first published in 2012. Sustainable innovation (*ijtihad*) is underpinned by an enlightened understanding and interpretation of Islamic discourse to address the current global issues and to find a common articulation and understanding of global commons like reconciliation, reconstruction, human emancipation, dignity and freedom.

Both environmental and technological determinism shape and frame our perceptions of space and time. The "island mindset" reflects a state of living and adapting to limited resources and coping with risks and uncertainties. It is also a good example of how human imagination is inspired by natural constraints. In many cases, physical constraints can be a driver for inspiration and innovation. I argue that the nation-state model is limiting opportunities for regional and global innovation.

The state of entropy, disorder or creative destruction in the socio-technological domain and at the political economy level is evident in many parts of the world including the Middle East and North Africa (MENA) region. Living in such a turbulent region raises a set of key questions, e.g., What does it mean to live in a troubled and entropic world like the MENA region in the twenty-first century? Can Science, Technology and Innovation (STI) pave a new avenue for a better future of progress and prosperity?

In this book, *Integral Innovation*, I attempt to transcend the boundaries of markets and governments to ecology, society and culture. The innovation journey in this book is framed by the "innovation-sustainability nexus". This book is informed, guided and inspired by the work of Lessem and Schieffer (2008; 2016). It is also a journey towards managing "creative destruction", reconstruction and renewal for an innovative nation, government, organization, city and individual. It is a purposeful attempt at reconstruction of an innovative ICON mind. This requires a deeper understanding of culture, ecology, technology and the national agenda for sustainable development.

One of the key questions that I attempt to explore is how nations acquire or lose their innovative capacity and what the conditions and enablers are for sustaining a culture of innovation in both organizations and nations. The *innovation-sustainability nexus* underpins the journey of innovation management in the domains of ideas, individuals, organizations and social structures. Reflecting on the cycles of history and the rise and fall of civilizations, we realize that innovation emerges after a state of deconstruction or an unsteady state of organizations and nations. Refugees play a vital role in innovation through swimming upstream. Paradoxically, Islamic civilization faced a set of challenges that hindered the sustainability of innovation and the culture of open innovation and societal reflection. Although the Islamic civilization had contributed to enlightenment and scientific discoveries in the Golden Age, the ecosystem, culture and social DNA of innovation is not deeply rooted in the local context in the twenty-first century.

I envision the community and/or city as a living laboratory for innovation. All ideas and interactions of people and organizations are manifested in our communities/cities. It would be illuminating to envision new innovative communities/cities in Damascus, Baghdad, Sanaa, Tripoli, Jerusalem and Gaza after a reconstruction that harnesses STI for the sake of a sustainable human civilization. I tend to use the analogy of the rebuilding of the city of Chicago after the fire in 1871 and the rebuilding of German and Japanese cities after World War II. The key questions outlined in this book are articulated as follows:

- Does the fall of nations, organizations and individuals indicate a lack or loss of *innovation capacity*? Is there a correlation between the rise of nations and organizations and the innovative climate and culture?

- How do we explain the fact that some countries with sound *infrastructure* for innovation systems are unable to move forwards?

- What are the necessary and sufficient *conditions* for evolving an innovative individual, community/city, organization or nation?

- Is there an *innovation determinism* that is linked to technological, cultural and environmental determinism?

- What can we learn from the innovation-sustainability nexus?

- Can we design an *education system* that has the capacity to instil a culture of innovation in a virtual and globalized world?

- How can history, culture, ecology and local knowledge define, frame and reform a new form of innovation beyond markets and firms?

- Can we envision a model for an innovative community/city that embodies the theory and practice of innovation?

- What are the projections beyond the knowledge economy and the innovation economy? Can we forecast the emergence of a new global consciousness that is in harmony with society, the economy and culture?

- Is there a continuity or a discontinuity in the four domains of innovations – i.e., ICON – and how can this issue be overcome?

Integral innovation is a purposeful effort to navigate through different types, forms and phases of innovation (social, ecological, institutional, technological and economic) to deepen our understanding of the DNA of social change, technical progress and sustainability. The interface between culture and innovation needs to be explored to unlock the human potential and value the contributions of all cultures and nations in the journey towards a sustainable future. In a nutshell, the prosperity of humankind is underpinned by our ability to embrace openness and celebrate diversity through the cross-fertilization and fusion of innovative ideas from all cultures.

While *civilization educates, culture enlightens* and hence we need to seek enlightenment for inducing innovation that is lodged in culture and ecology. Integral innovation implies the ability of seeing systems, networks and webs of life. The basic notion of *tawheed* in the Islamic worldview has immense applications for "systems" and unity in sciences (natural and social), unity in art and science, unity in human origin and destiny and unity in all cultures. This cosmic, human and ecological unity is a clear manifestation of the oneness of this integral innovation. Hence, human imagination and the holistic notions of innovation are inspired from the cosmos, ecology, culture and human history.

Integral innovation is simply about the *internet of ideas* and the web of cultures that shape science and technology to develop a sustainable future for humanity. I intend to look at the hidden connections and cycles in ecology, history and business to shed light on a possible newly emerging paradigm of integral innovation.

INNOVATION: A DEFINITION

Innovation means the successful exploitation of new ideas.

- *Innovation comes in many forms*: new or significantly improved products (goods or services), processes, marketing techniques, organizational methods in business practices, workplace organization or external relations all constitute forms of innovation.

- *Innovation does not only refer to radically new ideas*: radical and revolutionary innovation may have the greatest immediate societal impact, but new ideas do not have to be novel. An idea that is new to a firm rather than a new invention also counts as innovation – and can have significant benefits for that firm's productivity.

- *Innovation can mean adopting ideas from elsewhere*: innovation does not have to be devised in situ; the ability to draw on a variety of sources of knowledge and exploit ideas created in other city regions, universities and firms is critical.

- *Innovation is important to all sectors*: while often associated primarily with science and technology, innovation is, in fact, a major economic driver within all sectors of the economy.

Source: OECD. (2005). Oslo Manual: Guidelines for Collecting and Interpreting Innovation Data, Paris: OECD

In a market economy that views the value of the "world of things", we end up losing sight of the value of the "world of ideas". Economics has framed the current development model, but it is crucial that developmental thinking is reformed by ecology and culture.

Integral innovation is simply about the web of ecosystems and cultures that contribute to social, user and open innovations. In the current market-led economy, humans suffer from blind spots, nature deficit disorder and ecological amnesia; these human deficiencies limit our ability to capture value and inspiration from both ecology and culture. What seems to capture attention in the business books is "technical innovation" detached from, or not well aligned with, institutional and socio-cultural innovation at the macro-level.

Innovation is simply about seeing the missing links, making sense of them and acting on them; it is about harnessing the web of ideas from ecology and culture to add value and competitive advantage for nations, firms and individuals. This book is intended to deepen and broaden the notion of innovation to encompass culture, ecology and history. In an era of deep social and economic transformations, seeking inspiration for Islamic values and civilization is critical to reconciliation and to developing a unifying human consciousness and a new discourse for an alliance of civilizations which is underpinned by co-existence, human dignity, equity and human emancipation.

After the events of 2011, or what was called the "Arab Spring", which resulted in a state of instability and destruction in the MENA region, it is crucial to rethink and revisit the foundations of STI as a driver for prosperity and development. It is therefore imperative to harness the essence of innovation in all domains of life to enable individuals, organizations and societies to embody new worldviews for a sustainable human civilization based on adaptation, co-existence, resilience, reconciliation, tolerance, open and collective innovation and societal renewal. STI for sustainable development was viewed as a driving force and an overarching theme for the UN Post 2015 Agenda. However, innovative nations, organizations and individuals are key ingredients for transforming this vision into reality. The MENA region should be mindful of the role of STI in founding and nurturing sustainable organizations, cities, societies and nations through good governance, partnerships, civic intelligence and ethics.

Cities and communities are viewed as a living laboratory for innovation since they reflect the level of aligning and harnessing the financial capital with social, natural, manufactured and intellectual capitals. Our human collective efforts will be fruitful in integral innovation when we are able to revive and reconstruct the smart Arab cities in Gulf Cooperation Council (GCC) countries and in turbulent states like Yemen, Syria, Libya, Iraq, Palestine and Sudan. The ability to organize the built environment in the public and private institutions, infrastructure, services and STI should be part of a transformative vision to move beyond the state of *creative destruction* to one of *innovative reconstruction*. Refugees, as has always been the case in Europe and the USA, should be viewed as an opportunity, a new ingredient and a driving force for socio-eco-innovation, rather than a threat or risk. The influx of refugees in all parts of the world represents a state of "bounded instability" to introduce new insights for integral innovation, global governance, business models, new consciousness and leadership.

This book is about the co-development of an innovative ICON, an essential ingredient and enabler for renewal and enlightenment. The first chapter reviews the key components of integral innovation which is a manifestation of the internet of ideas that includes history, society, ecology, economy, technology, cities and organizations. Chapters 2 through 5 address each component of the multi-dimensional model of innovation which entails innovations inspired and framed by society, ecology, history and culture.

In this chapter, I intend to set the scene for a conceptual model that frames integral innovation. I argue that framing the notion of integral innovation is critical to developing new insights into innovation beyond markets and competition. An innovation model that encompasses history, ecology and society, policy and practice, and the nation and community/city is the focus of this book. A set of dimensions of innovation are conceptualized, constructed and articulated to develop a new model for transformative innovation for societies and organizations. These dimensions of integral innovation are presented and outlined below:

- Cultural/social innovation;

- Eco-innovation;

- Technological innovation;

- Economic/ business innovation.

1.3 Cultural/social innovation

Reviving the essence and inspiration of local culture is key to rooting integral innovation in the MENA and GCC regions. The palm tree and oud plant are the sources for two iconic business in the GCC and worldwide. Bateel palm dates and Arabian oud-based perfumes are shining examples of cultural innovation.

Cultural innovation is key to nurturing local roots and social DNA for innovation since I believe that while civilization educates, culture enlightens. The post-colonial era in many developing countries resulted in the dislocation of reference frames and the emergence of divergent and sub-identities and sub-cultures. Striking the right balance between Western technique and Eastern values, and between the religious and secular, remains a challenge for reviving models for socio-technological innovation and instilling a culture of innovation at all levels.

The historical initiatives in the nineteenth century for reform and renewal in the MENA region emphasized both cultural and technological innovations. The future of the GCC and MENA region is underpinned by the ability to articulate a new discourse for an "innovative culture" along with evolving an institutional and technological infrastructure and an ecosystem for STI. The innovation-sustainability nexus implies the need to define key conditions related to renewal and innovation to form an identity and a sense of unity within global diversity and to revitalize a renewed Islamic discourse that deepens and contextualizes the notion of a "median community" (*ummah wassat*) that celebrates co-existence, cultural diversity and integral innovation.

Integral innovation requires the embodiment of an eco-cosmic ethos and a new educational system that balances *spiritual, ecological and cultural dimensions* including art, local knowledge and heritage. It also implies accepting differences as a source of enrichment, resilience and vitality. On the other hand, integral innovation is fuelled by both ecological and cultural diversity to frame and define local, regional and global commons to achieve public interest and collective rational actions. In a globalized world that sees potential risks due to poverty, disease, unemployment, climate change, energy security and refugees, it is insightful to harness and unlock this human capital for innovative forces that can transform scarcity to abundance and challenges and risks to opportunities.

An enabler and a cornerstone for cultural renewal is transformative education that focuses on design thinking. The innovative education system is the bedrock for socio-technological transformation. However, the history of civilizations in the field of STI is documented in a selective and cross-sectional fashion. Meri (2005) noted that there is an absence of dialogue about the historical legacy of Islamic civilization in Western formal education. Hence, it is imperative to co-create proper platforms that nurture diversity and celebrate the collective cross-cultural contributions in human civilization.

Traditional education systems frame minds to tell the story that a local culture or nation represents the core and the rest, or the "other", is the peripheral. This mono-cultural education frames the human mind in a polarized manner and limits space for *cultural innovation*. Fruitful cultural interaction and cross-fertilization are essential to help future generations appreciate the collective contributions of all nations. This global education is likely to inspire new ways of thinking, knowing and doing. Hence, the strategic intent for a model of integral innovation is to support global education that is enabled to inspire minds to embrace co-existence, diversity, tolerance and peace.

Cultural innovation is enriched and informed through learning about other cultures and languages. The richness in cultures offers possibilities for interaction, understanding and the fusion of ideas that informs many forms of innovation. In fact, each culture brings new viewpoints and perspectives that may induce non-linear, dynamic, interactive, radical and open innovation models. Adopting new modes of learning and reflection, with reconstruction and reformation of the local knowledge, is critical to making a clear distinction between the two divergent meanings for innovation in the Arabic culture, i.e., deviation (*bed'a*) and innovation (*ijtihad*). This divergent perception of the two meanings of innovation requires deeper exploration to reconstruct a new discourse of innovation.

The deeper realization of the essence of innovation is manifested in the history of science and technology. It was a process of selective assimilation of knowledge from Greece, Rome and India that enabled Islamic civilization to flourish. In addition, the notion of innovation that is inspired from culture and local knowledge constitutes a cornerstone in the Islamic worldview which sees that both physical and spiritual knowledge are key ingredients for eco-imagination, open innovation and inspiration from ecology, history and culture.

The unity in knowledge and reasoning was evident in the work of Rushd (1954). The seeds of hope for nurturing an "innovative mind" come through exploration, inquiry, application of reasoning and dialogue between philosophy and religion. In an attempt to revisit the foundations of Islamic culture, Iqbal in his work *The Reconstruction of Religious Thought in Islam* (1986) argued that Islamic revolutionary thought was founded on an intellectual imperative and mandate to remove the dichotomy between revelation and state authority and between the religious and the secular domains of knowledge. Harmony in these domains is critical for realizing an innovative nation, organization and individual.

The intellectual contribution of Iqbal in this seminal work about the *reconstruction of Islamic thought* sheds light on the conditions that were necessary for the enlightenment and reformation in Europe which inspired the Industrial Revolution (Iqbal 1986). According to Iqbal, the birth of the Islamic worldview symbolizes the initiation of inductive intellectual reasoning and scientific inquiry. He argued that there is a need to revisit and critique the Western worldview with respect to the essence of biology and economics. In addition, he called for an enlightened process of revisiting and reflecting on Islam in the light of modern scientific knowledge in biology, chemistry, quantum physics and space, as articulated by Guessoum (2012).

A key ingredient of the "intellectual revolution", as argued by Iqbal, is to contextualize the notion of *tawheed* and eradicate all forms of injustice and human exploitation through transformative education so as to induce a state of metamorphosis in mind and soul. In essence, the inner world of man should be enlightened to transcend to a state of "inner beauty" (*ihsan*). Islam teaches that people must change from within before they can change the external environment. Iqbal (1986) argued: "It is this internal and psychological revolution in the personalities of individual human beings that is the absolutely essential pre-requisite for any meaningful and stable change in the politico-socio-economic system".

In the twenty-first century, there is still a need for an innovative reading of local knowledge, culture and heritage in light of the globalized market economy, social relativism and the commodification of cultures. Social, cultural, open and user innovation can offer new possibilities for addressing core issues related to poverty, governance, human health, resource depletion, financial deficit, refugees and climate change.

The history of technological innovation is simply the narrative of humankind pursuing a good, safe, efficient and comfortable life. As mentioned previously, the term "innovation" is also translated in the Arabic language as *bed'a* which refers to a negative cultural meaning that implies a deviation from the fundamental roots of Islamic values, which further implies a static stagnation of ideas if the concept is extrapolated to encompass all domains of intellectual inquiry.

The modern Muslim in the twenty-first century cannot live on the legacy of the past by referring to the *Golden Age* as a source of inspiration and as testimony to the Islamic contribution to European Renaissance. What is needed is a fresh and deeper understanding and analysis of the conditions for progress and prosperity.

After salient historical transitions, it is imperative for individuals, organizations and nations to revisit their worldviews, business models or paradigms to leapfrog into a better future. In this book, the overarching theme is that innovation is underpinned by intellectual, institutional and cultural contexts. Hence, any attempt to instil a culture of innovation will not be fruitful unless it is lodged and rooted in history, culture, ecology and epistemology. After the colonial era the Muslim world went through a process of rethinking and reflection on the roots of technical change and prosperity. This was reflected in the writings of Mohammad Iqbal (1986) where he emphasized the role of reason, deduction, induction and innovation in addressing socio-technological transformations. The pressing question is how organizations and nations overcome the inertia and stagnation in the world of ideas and apply an innovative process to the reconstruction of minds and the built environment.

It seems to me that it will be insightful to conceptualize the *thermodynamics* not the *statics* of innovation which are embedded in *knowledge flows* and energy transfer not in the *quantity of data*. In addition, innovation matters because it is concerned with the *direction of progress* rather than the *content of progress*. I see innovation in a multi-dimensional space and time that encompasses all

RENEWAL AS A CONDITION FOR SUSTAINABILITY

The basic notion in the Islamic worldview that there is a process of intellectual, cultural and social reformers and change agents inducing a transformative change in society (*mujaddidoun*) is illuminating and inspiring. This implies there are continuous dynamic forces that instill a sense of hope, optimism and energy to create change and celebrate obsolescence of old ideas, methods and ways of thinking, knowing and doing. The key question is how we manage and accept this flux of renewal in all aspects of life.

human endeavours for the pursuit of a good, sustainable and resilient life. In other words, innovation is a collective societal worldview that is informed and fuelled by leadership, governance and vision. This vision is embedded in philosophy and culture which is a form of positive and renewable energy available for the transformation of ICONs. I intend to base the following chapters on the four elements included in ICON as drivers and enablers and *hardware* of the integral innovation model as shown in Figure 1.1.

However, in many developing countries there is a disconnect between the four pillars of innovation as captured in ICON at one level and at another level there is also disconnect at the core as manifested in the dislocation of culture and ecology from technical and economic innovation due to the linking of modernization with Westernization during the colonial era. These two systemic and structural barriers limit the propensity to innovate, which is a function of individual traits, enabling community/city environment, organizational culture and national vision. The intensity and velocity of the "flow of innovation" across the two domains (ICON and CETE) are critical for sustainable integral innovation as shown in Figure 1.1.

Despite the cultural belief in the Islamic worldview that there is a cycle of renewal at the rise of every century, there is no consensus on who the recognized agents of change (*mujadiddoun*) are throughout Islamic civilization. This raises the important question of what constitutes innovation within a broader historical, socio-technological context. Moreover, it is illuminating to design an enabling environment for purposeful integral innovation to enlighten ICONs. Design thinking in education and socio-technical transformation should be utilized to plan and manage integral innovation at all levels of society.

There is an illuminating story about Prophet Mohammad (peace be upon him) where he commented on the methods for cross-fertilization of palm trees in Medina (the first city founded in Islam) in the form of a question on the local practices and knowledge. When the local community applied the Prophet's advice, the palm trees did not flourish as expected. The Prophet commented: "You are more aware of what is good for your daily matters". The morale of this narrative is to make a clear distinction between two domains of knowledge: the constant (*thabit*) and variable (*mutaghyer*) forms of knowledge. In the twenty-first century, the Muslim community (*ummah*) needs to make a clear distinction between the limits of these domains of knowledge, about the balance between stability and change.

Making a distinction between the two domains of knowledge is the key to resolving the on-going debate on the reference point for judgment and rulings in all matters including political consensus, economic reform, environmental conservation and technological innovation. The two schools of knowledge, the mind (*aql*) and the text (*naql*), are in a state of flux in the pursuit of defining and redefining what constitutes goodness, rightness and beauty and what makes a sustainable and innovative ICON. The human worldview is shaped by evidence and wisdom extracted from historical and cultural contexts and realities.

Decolonizing and reconstructing the mind are key pre-requisites for innovation and enlightenment in the Arab world. One of the scholars who addressed this challenge is Al-Jabri, a philosopher from Morocco. Al-Jabri (2011) critically commented and reflected on heritage in terms of structure, history and ideology. He conceptualized that thought is framed and determined by two things: the field of knowledge and the ideological content. The first implies the field in which thought moves, which is composed of the material of knowledge and a thinking apparatus. The second implies the possible social and political functions that thought has. Such a reading, according to Al-Jabri (2011), provides an alternative to those other readings that emphasized either the material of knowledge or the ideological content.

Al-Jabri (2011) argued that there was an *epistemological break* between the philosophers of the East and the Islamic Empire and those of North Africa (Andalusia and Morocco). This epistemological break can be seen in the writings of Ibn Hazm, al-Shatibi and Ibn Khaldun. More importantly, he developed a genealogy of the main ideas present in Arabic thought in the classical period which includes the three epistemological systems of indication (*bayan*), illumination (`*irfan*) and demonstration (*burhan*). For Al-Jabri the epistemological system of indication was, historically, the earliest within Arab thought. It had become dominant in the so-called indigenous sciences like jurisprudence and legal system (*fiqh*), Quranic sciences (interpretations, hermeneutics and exegesis), theology, and non-philosophical literary theory. Indication started out being a combination of rules for interpreting discourse and determining the conditions of discourse production.

The overall result was a theory of knowledge that was explicatory (*bayani*) at all levels. He also arrived at a conclusion that the system of explication is governed by the two principles of separation or discontinuation (*infisal*) and possibility or contingency (*tajwiz*). These principles are manifested in the theory of the individual substance which maintains that the relationship between individual substances is based upon contiguity and association, but not influence and interaction.

In his work entitled *Critique of Arab Political Reason*, Al-Jabri (2011) adopted the "social imaginary" to define the key determinants and notions that shape the traditional Arab mind as manifested in the current state of the MENA: the tribe (*qabilah*), the spoils or plunder (*al-ghanimah*) and the faith (*al-'aqidah*). However, the dichotomy between the religious and secular schools of thought appeared vividly in countries such as Egypt, Tunisia, Yemen, Libya and Syria after the Arab Spring. This

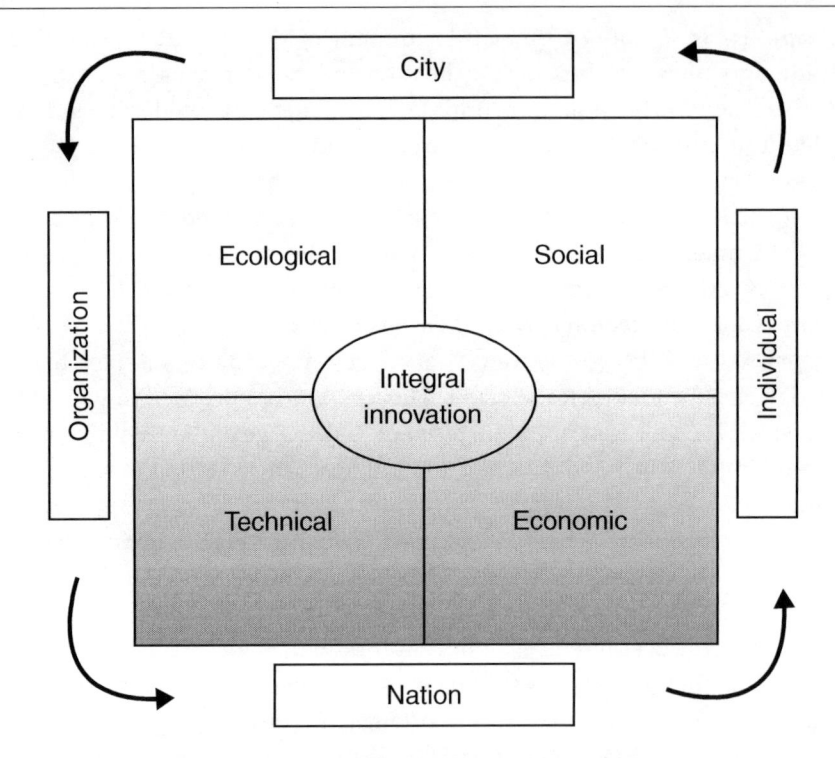

Figure 1.1   A conceptual framework for integral innovation

in turn resulted in *disruptive, entropic and chaotic* unsteady states in the MENA region that require new reconstruction through a new innovative journey. The departure from such a state requires an integral innovation system at the individual, organizational, city-governance and national levels to embody social/cultural, ecological, economic and technological innovations as depicted in Figure 1.1.

1.4 Ecological innovation

Every living organism in this planet is an open source for learning and innovation. The key challenge is to develop an enlightened education system and the human capacity to learn from nature and apply this knowledge to business, city and community. Ecology is a source of inspiration and innovation since it generates energy and new resources for life through photosynthesis. Industries and organizations are developing innovations by mimicking nature. The key question is to what extent our organizations and businesses are capable of harnessing the open source of knowledge and innovation that is inspired by nature, i.e., eco-innovation. In a digitized world where consumers wait in long queues to purchase a new iPhone when it is released, there is a risk of a deepened state of "nature deficit disorder" and ecological amnesia unless innovative technologies are aligned and informed by ecology.

A sustainable society, community or ecology needs an accurate balance sheet that reflects the status of the ecosystem services and enhances the flow of financial, manufactured, human and natural capital. The current economic metrics do not account for the value and benefit of the ecosystem services. The key to sustainability according to Lovins, Lovins and Hawken (1999) is to seek to fully harness all four capital stockholdings (financial and manufactured, natural and human). It is believed that the next revolution, after the digital revolution, will be an ecological one. The key implications and requirements for this ecological revolution include increased resource productivity, enhancement of flow and services and reduction or elimination of waste. Reducing and eliminating the very idea of waste can be accomplished by redesigning technology and industry on the principles of ecology and biology. This means changing the nature of industrial processes and materials, enabling the newly sustainable society to maintain and develop a constant use of materials in continuous closed circles. This entails a new perception of value and a shift from the acquisition of goods to the purchase of services, whereby quality, utility and performance are continually sought to promote natural and social wellbeing.

Mainstream sustainable development, according to Adams and Jeanrenaud (2008), encompasses a series of ideas such as *ecological modernization* and *market environmentalism* that promise to steer the world towards sustainability in ways that do not demand too many dramatic changes. Green innovations were driven by legal or policy constraints to minimize the ecological footprints and pollution. Such innovations may entail enhancement of resource efficiency or changes in business models, paradigms, products, designs or processes. The "green economy" concept is a developmental model that supports green businesses and small and medium enterprises (SMEs) to harness and capture innovations from ecology. This in turn is inducing a shift in the business model and innovations along the supply chain.

In this perspective, sustainable development can therefore best be achieved through "fostering economic growth and development, while ensuring that natural assets continue to provide the resources and environmental services on which our well-being relies" (Morrow, 2012; Strange and Bayley, 2008), by emphasizing "environmentally sustainable economic progress to foster low-carbon, socially inclusive development" (Morrow, 2012; ADB, UNEP and UNESCAP, 2012).

The notion of the green economy entails the development of green jobs and green growth. The "green economy in the context of sustainable development and poverty eradication" (Kazzi, 2014) carries the promise of a new economic growth paradigm that is friendly to the earth's ecosystems while also contributing to poverty alleviation as illustrated in Figure 1.2.

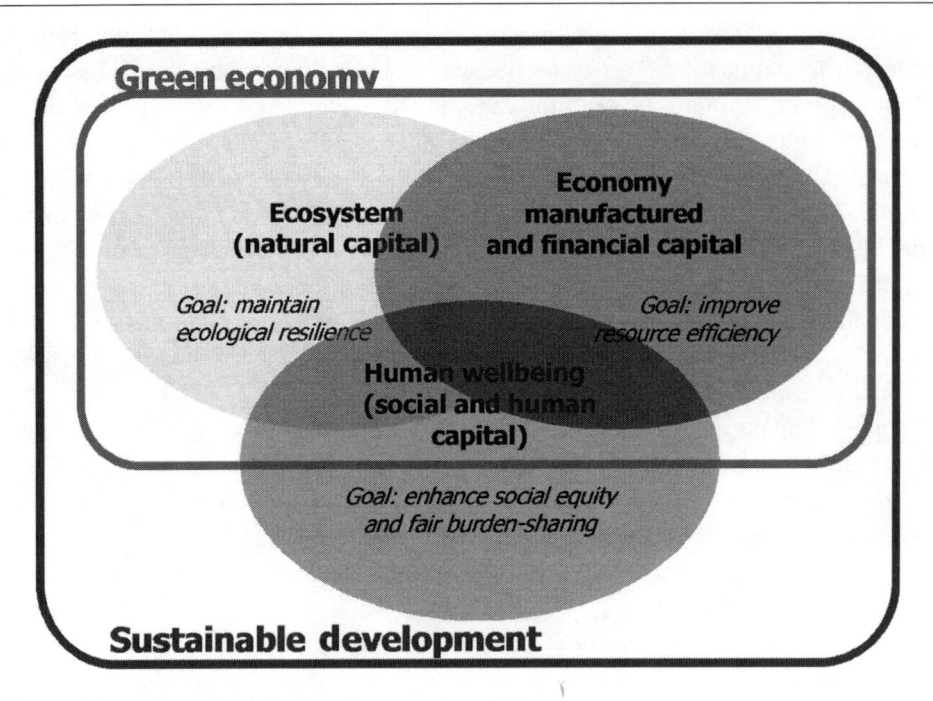

Figure 1.2 Sustainable development and the green economy

Both the green economy and green growth offer a novel approach for the innovation-sustainability nexus. Both "should be understood as identifying and supporting opportunities to improve natural resource management and provide infrastructure services while meeting the core objectives of human development and well-being" (Kazzi, 2014). The green economy therefore balances the needs of *people*, the *planet*, and *profits* by reconciling the *environment* (planet), where humans live, with the *economy* (profits) and the system of activities that they undertake to improve their *standard of living* (people).

Green technology is viewed as the manufactured capital that can contribute to three domains of sustainability through improving efficiency as in the case of water saving devices, technology for irrigation management and monitoring, and technologies of energy efficiency, renewable energy and climate change. Also, green technology can contribute to enhancing ecological resilience as in the case of technologies used to monitor the quality of water, air and soil, and water treatment and wastewater reuse technologies. It is inspiring to witness a new discourse in media and policy circles that views nature and ecosystems as a source of inspiration as manifested in research on green business, hybrid-cars, eco-innovation and bio-innovation. This has also been evident in the global media, for example on the BBC and CNN in their documentaries like *Nature Inc.* and *Green Business.*

In addition, the economics and politics of climate change and the scale and speed of natural degradation and species extinction reveal that humans suffer from ecological amnesia and nature deficit disorder (Al-Jayyousi, 2016). A critical element in improving or enhancing the productivity of ecosystem services (*natural capital*) is ecological conservation and restoration. The natural capital underpins both the social and financial capitals. However, technology (*manufactured capital*) can be designed to enhance and support the natural and social capitals through sound application of technologies in education, governance, rural development, water, environment, agriculture, energy and health. For example, in the field of agriculture, biodiversity provides the genetic variability from wild relatives of domestic plants and animals that enables farmers to continually improve the food supplies upon which we depend and from which scientists develop biotechnology to enhance productivity.

Renewable energy including hydro-power, solar, wind, bio-fuels, bio-energy and energy from waste are becoming increasingly important in providing energy security and contributing to the alleviation of climate change risks. Desalination technology is critical for GCC countries to ensure water security. Wastewater reuse technologies are adopted in many countries to augment and enhance water supply. Traditional and local knowledge like decentralized water and wastewater treatment plants are used to serve small communities and refugees. All these technological innovations are paving the way to making optimum use of informatics and telecommunication systems to address environmental sustainability, water and air monitoring, climate risks and natural disasters. The concept of the right to access information and open sources addresses today's needs and promotes active participation in decision making.

In sum, the shift in global environmental and climate change policy and green activism are shaping global development policy. Green business and arguments for a green economy represent a new discourse to address market failures. A low-carbon economy, de-growth and a circular economy are new emerging models that aspire to achieve prosperity without growth. A transition to a green economy achieved global consensus in the Paris Climate Change Summit in 2015. This global commitment is a testimony to a potential macro-shift that has substantial implications in the economy and society as a whole. As a result, a shift to renewable energy, green technology and eco-innovations is shaping a new development agenda for the future. In sum, the eco-innovation paradigm requires new learning models, processes and practices to transfer eco-knowledge to organizations, cities and society.

1.5 Technological innovation

Transforming an idea into a product or a process through commercializing and marketing underpins the concept of innovation. This requires a business model innovation along with an institutional innovation, an ecosystem and an enabling environment for creativity, invention and innovation. Technology can speed up and facilitate an incremental or radical innovation as in the Skype case study illustrated below.

Historically, the notion of technology underwent shifts from focusing on *tools* to *knowledge* to *culture*. The emergence of the human civilization has been closely connected to the development of appropriate technology in infrastructure for water, energy, transport and agriculture. After the Industrial Revolution, it was considered that science and technology could solve all social and economic issues. Later, it was realized that we need to develop ethics in science and technology to manage the spillover effects of technology like nuclear technology and other environmental externalities such as climate change, pollution and waste. Nevertheless, emerging technologies in the era of cloud computing and the "internet of things" are likely to enhance efficiency and productivity substantially through innovations in renewable energy, biotechnology, medicine, nanotechnology and ecological systems. In essence, STI are underpinned by social choices, hence a transition to a sustainable green economy is simply about the redefinition of STI policy and development agendas. In doing so, it is important to examine closely the historical context for STI in the East and West.

The globe experienced a set of macro-shifts in worldviews, knowledge and technology that affected society, economy and ecology and, hence, introduced a variety of notions of progress and modernism throughout history. These historical benchmarks include the Era of Renaissance (1400–1500), the Age of Exploration and Colonization (1500–1800), the Scientific Revolution (1600–1700), the Age of Enlightenment (1700–1800), and the Industrial Revolution (1750–1900).

The establishment of universities in the tenth century in Paris, Naples and Oxford created a new reference and space for critical thinking, logical reasoning and debate. This resulted in deep hope and optimism in the potential role of science and technology in solving all human challenges which is viewed as the foundation for European Enlightenment. The famous German theologian Albertus Magnus (1193–1280) and Thomas Aquinas (1225–1274) argued for the concept of combining Greek philosophy with religion and the idea of multiple paths to realizing the truth through observation, reasoning and logic. Aquinas sought to find a middle point between the rationalism of Aristotle and the Christian faith. This launched the era of philosophical dualism, an idea which is based on rational and naturalistic ideas of Greek philosophy and Christian faith.

However, during this era (1200 AD), Islamic civilization was experiencing a rise in STI via an exchange of ideas from India and China through trade. As argued by many scholars of the history of science, the reintroduction of Greek philosophy and science to European thinking can be attributed to the Islamic civilization. This era witnessed remarkable inventions like the compass, mechanical clock, gunpowder and the printing press.

The exploration of America and the Protestant Reformation movement in the sixteenth century paved the way for a new era of modernism. These events had a salient impact on the perception of space, history, society, economy and intellectual movement in Europe. In addition, the competition between Spain, England, France and Portugal fuelled innovation in navigational and military technology. This era witnessed a new notion of astronomy and space when Nicolaus Copernicus (1473–1543) stated his famous theory that the earth was not the centre of the universe but actually revolved around the sun. This marked the beginnings of modern physical science in opposition to the authority of Aristotle, and openly challenged the authority of Genesis as a correct account of the origin and nature of the universe. Moreover, Johannes Kepler (1571–1630), co-inventor of the telescope, discovered the laws of planetary motion, further reinforcing Copernicus' theory, as well as setting the stage for Isaac Newton's grand scientific synthesis later in the century. Although the historical development of science can be traced through the ideas of the ancient Greeks, the investigations and studies of Islamic scholars, and the writings of Bacon, among others, modern science was born in the sixteenth and seventeenth centuries.

These technological innovations opened a new approach for understanding, knowing and reasoning. The rational theory of science, scientific method and the meaning of progress were redefined and articulated by Sir Francis Bacon

> **WHAT IS PROGRESS?**
>
> The historian Robert Nisbet asserts that progress is the most important idea ever developed in Western civilization. He identifies five basic premises behind the modern secular theory of progress: the value of the past, the superiority of the West, the worth of economic and technological growth, faith in reason and science, and the importance of life on earth. The philosophy of secular progress as it developed in the modern West assumed that progress is cumulative, building upon the accomplishments of the past; that the West should take a leadership position as the most modernized culture and society in the world; and that economic and technological developments facilitate advances in all *spheres of human reality*.

(1561–1626) and Rene Descartes (1596–1650). While Bacon argued that humanity could improve natural reality, as well as human society, through the application of scientific knowledge, Descartes believed that scientific knowledge should be built upon rational deductions. On the other hand, Newton argued that the universe was fundamentally a machine; hence both nature and human society could be viewed as machines and manipulated to serve human ends.

Interestingly, in the midst of increased openness and competition among different points of view, one theory emerged that came to dominate early thinking in science. The Scientific Revolution culminated in Sir Isaac Newton's (1642–1727) theory of mechanics, motion and gravitation which seemed to provide a comprehensive scientific explanation of a perceived physical universe.

The Scientific Revolution found order within the changing world of nature and time. What Newton retained from Plato was that this order in nature was imposed by an eternal reality. Newton believed that the beauty and orderliness of nature must be due to a supreme being, the Creator.

Robert Nisbet suggests that the Western view of progress includes several key features: the value of the past, the worth of economic and technological growth, faith in reason and science, and the importance of life on earth. Also, Leibniz proposed a theory of universal progress where he argued that *the* infinite progress of the universe is the realization of the perfection and beauty of God – the creator of the universe.

In sum, the history of science and technology was part of the Western search for the systems that govern nature and humans. This journey resulted in a separation of science and religion, and state and religion. However, this dichotomy does not, and should not, exist in the Middle Eastern or Islamic worldview, since the trajectory of science and technology did not suffer from the Western syndrome of separation; instead it is about *tawheed*. The linkage or correlation between innovation and cultural values needs to be explored and examined to dispel the hypothesis that religious beliefs pose constraints on human innovative capacity. This misunderstanding is attributed to the association of modernization and reformation with Westernization which is part of the colonization legacy. Integral innovation from an Islamic worldview resonates with notions of unity, coherence and value creation.

1.6 CASE STUDY 1.1: THE DISRUPTIVE BUSINESS MODEL OF SKYPE

Skype successfully combined two emerging technologies to create a new service and business model for telecommunications. The two technologies were Voice over Internet Protocol (VoIP) and peer-to-peer (P2P) file sharing. The first allowed the transfer of voice over the Internet rather than conventional telecommunications networks, and the other exploited the distributed computing power of users' computers to avoid the need for a dedicated centralized server or infrastructure.

Skype was created in 2003 by the Swedish serial entrepreneur Nikias Zennstrom, who was previously (in)famous for his pioneering web company Kazaa, which provided a P2P service, mainly used for the (illegal) exchange of MP3 music files. He sold Kazaa to the US company Sharman Networks to concentrate on the development of Skype. He teamed up with the Dane Janus Friis and together they built Skype. Unlike other VoIP firms like Vonage, which charges a subscription for use and is based on proprietary hardware, Skype was available for free download and use for free voice communication between computers. Additional premium pay services were subsequently added such as Skype-Out to connect to conventional telephones and Skype-In to receive conventional calls. The service was made available in fifteen different languages which covered 165 countries and partnerships were made with Plantronics to provide headsets and Siemens and Motorola for handsets.

Given the provision of free software and free calls between computers, the business model had to be innovative. There were several ways in which revenues were generated. The premium services like Skype-In and Skype-Out proved to be very popular with small- and medium-sized firms for business and conference calls, and the licensing of the software to specialist providers and the hardware partnership deals were also lucrative. Later, the large user base also attracted web advertising.

By 2005, there were 70 million users registered but despite this rapid growth the core model of providing a free service meant that revenues were a rather more modest US$7 million, equivalent to only 10 cents per user. In 2008 Skype had around 310 million registered users 12 million of which were online at any time. Its revenues were estimated to be US$126 million, equivalent to 40 cents per user. This does represent an improvement in financial performance, especially as costs remain low, but the business model remains unproven except for the founders of Skype. They sold the company to eBay in October 2005 who plan to use Skype to increase trading turnover by introducing voice bargaining and pay-per-call advertising and exploit their previous acquisition PayPal to provide improved billing for Skype customers.

Source: Adapted from Rao B. Angelov (2006) Fusion of disruptive technologies lessons from the Skype case. European Management Journal 24 (2 & 3) 174–188.

1.7 Economic/business innovation

The history of innovation is closely linked to economic theory and technical change after World War II. Joseph Schumpeter (1883–1950) combined insights from economics, sociology and history to study the role of innovation in social change. His focus was on the interaction of innovative individuals and their social surroundings and the role of R&D in innovation. Later, Research and Development Corporation (RAND) studied the outcomes and factors that affect innovation in the USA as documented by Arrow (1962) and Nelson (1959). The work of Nelson (1962) titled *The Rate and Direction of Inventive Activities* addressed key questions including the sources of innovation and the role of science in R&D. The publications of Freeman and colleagues on *Unemployment and Technical Innovation* (Freeman, Clark and Soete, 1982) and *The Economics of the Industrial Innovation* (Freeman, 1982; Freeman and Soete, 1997) were a substantial contribution to the theory of innovation through the Science Policy Research Unit at the University of Sussex. Freeman's contributions reveal correlations between innovation and economic growth and organizational learning. Later, the concept of a national system of innovation was developed to take into account the social, institutional and political dimensions as articulated by Lundvall (1992) and Nelson (1993).

The concept of innovation in many developing countries is closely linked to invention and imported products. The post-colonial era in the Middle East resulted in a model of dependency and

> **ABDEEN INDUSTRIAL: A MODEL OF INNOVATION IN THE MIDDLE EAST**
>
> Mohamad Saeed Abdeen was a refugee who was forced to leave his own homeland Ramleh in Palestine in 1948 after the war. He was only a teenager when he was faced with this tragic event. The 1948 war forced the family to flee to Salt City in Jordan where his father started a small grocery store. In a few years this business had become a well-known supermarket in Amman City. The talented and innovative Mohamad had a passion for mechanics and industry. He was keen to start something new and be the first to introduce innovation to the market. He decided to change the family business into a small industry which initially traded in tools for grocery stores, beginning with the mechanical weighing balance. He had a chance to visit industrial museums in Germany which opened his mind to new ideas for the market. After about three decades the business had become one of the most successful SMEs in manufacturing display refrigerators in Jordan. His two sons, educated in the UK as engineers, later helped him grow the business, making it more structured and regional. This is the story of many SMEs founded by refugees in the MENA region. The key to sustainable business according to Mr Abdeen is hard work, honesty and integrity.

the dislocation of values from technology and development. This in turn caused a split of knowledge in the education system, i.e.; secular versus religious and natural and social sciences. The early urban centres in the Middle East, including Damascus, Baghdad, Jerusalem, Sana'a, Cairo and Tunisia, were flagships for knowledge creation, synthesis and enlightenment. An innovative city/community is a vivid manifestation of good governance, leadership, institutions and innovation. With ICT and globalization, global innovation models are emerging as a result of the convergence of ideas between cultures.

The cross-fertilization of cultures and fusion of ideas from Central Asia and the Far East, India, Rome and Greece made the Islamic culture fertile, innovative and resilient. Saliba (1999) argued that Renaissance scientists were open to using ideas from the Islamic world, which in turn contributed to the emergence of the twelfth-century Renaissance. However, Saliba (2000) commented that the concept of patents for new scientific and technological ideas was born in Europe and was an idea totally alien to non-European cultures. While the East pursued science for the intellectual pursuit and joy of knowledge, the West sought science as a means to wealth and capital creation through the development of intellectual property rights.

The basic model for depicting innovation consists of R&D, commercialization and diffusion. Although there is correlation between R&D expenditure and level of innovation, the linear model of innovation does not explain the complexity of innovation, hence, a number of models include interaction, coupling, network and open innovation.

1.8 Innovation enablers, drivers and imperatives

There is a belief in Islamic culture that each century witnesses one reformer (*mujadid*) who will renew discourse and trajectory. This renewal (*tajdeed*) process is vital for the notion of cultural and intellectual innovation to ensure a resilient and sustainable human civilization. Also, such a process entails a rethinking of the way individuals, organizations, communities and nations think, know and innovate to avoid stagnation and decadence. There is a consensus that Omar bin Abd Al-Aziz was the first to contribute to the renewal process through instilling a culture of social dialogue among divergent viewpoints to reach social consensus. Al-Shafe'y was the second scholar to establish and formalize system thinking and defining foundations for achieving public interest.

However, there is no consensus on who are considered the *innovators and leaders of renewals* in the centuries beyond the second century. This divergence of views has major ramifications on how societies see and value the "world of ideas" throughout space and time. There is a need not only to draw a historical profile for innovators, but also to design and predict the areas and gaps that mandate innovation for the future. The inability to agree on the change agents in Islamic history is attributed to the partial and fragmented view of innovation. Some tend to see innovation only in one discipline: the intellectual, social, institutional, scientific, ecological or economic/business realm.

Another challenge at the conceptual level is the fragmentation of knowledge and disciplines as a result of the Western conflict between the State and Church on the source of knowledge. The unity, or *tawheed*, in knowledge from an Islamic worldview between secular and religious views reconciles this dichotomy.

In a scientific forum in 2015, I was asked if scientific innovation should be detached from belief, faith and spirituality. My simple response was that all the key scientific advances in the Golden Age were undertaken by scientists who were believers in the Creator. The confusion stems from the debate and history of science that was elaborated earlier. This debate creates a sense of uncertainty and instability which defines a divergence in mental models between East and West. In essence, all forms and types of innovations are inspired and informed by a web of imagination, metaphors and analogies that are resourced by local knowledge, transcendent belief, culture, history and ecology.

Hence, there is no disconnect between the belief in the *tawheed* of God and technological innovation since it is imperative to be mindful of the "systems" that govern species, planet, humans and nature. In reality, what is important to note is that the Islamic conception of God as argued by Bausani (1974) made possible a major advance in scientific thinking during the period of the eighth to the fifteenth centuries in Islamic lands until the fall of Constantinople in 1453. The same mental models are poised to launch a new era of enlightenment.

At the social level, according to Algerian thinker, moral philosopher and educationalist Malek Bennabi (1988), all civilizations arise as a result of a religious principle which articulates the contours of civilization. In Islam, this phase corresponded to the prophetic period and its immediate aftermath. It culminated in what he called "the age of spirit". As the civilization expands, it also increases in complexity and resources, opening the second stage of the civilizational process, "the age of reason". This phase weakens the original religious impulse, and society begins to lose its commitment to the moral precepts of the religious base, even as it extends itself materially and intellectually. Societal bonds gradually unravel, ending the civilizational cycle.

Bennabi (1988) argued for the need to maintain the local identity of the Islamic civilization and to be aware of uncritical horizontal transfer of Western norms and worldviews. He called for the development of an aesthetic sensibility in the Muslim mind and spirit. To him, "pride in craftsmanship, deep knowledge in professions, development of a learning organization, reflective practitioners, attention to detail, diligence and perseverance, were the essential preconditions for the successful transplantation of modern knowledge into the Muslim world". All of these attributes are essential for nurturing a culture and climate of innovation at all levels and domains.

In the convergence between East and West, each culture has a value in the global alliance for innovation. Cross-fertilization among cultures is the cornerstone for integral innovation. Islamic civilization can be characterized as the preserver and then transmitter of the sciences and philosophies of the ancient Greeks to pre-Renaissance Europe through the Muslim-dominated, but cosmopolitan, centres of learning in Spain such as Toledo and Cordoba. The Muslims themselves had developed an advanced understanding of the physical and life sciences; they were versed in different fields such as mathematics, astronomy, optics and the entire spectrum of the medical arts and sciences. The pursuit of scientific goals was encouraged as part of the overall quest of mankind to see and affirm the signs of God in nature. The historian of Islamic science Seyyed Nasr (2003) wrote:

> *Unity between art and science is key for innovation. Islamic science came into being from a wedding between the spirit that issued from the Quranic revelation and the existing sciences of various civilizations. Islamic medicine was based on the assertion that the human body was a microcosmic reflection of the cosmos and that a balanced interrelationship between mind, body and spirit was essential to maintaining the health and vigour of the person. Islam recognized above all that the domain of the infinite, of boundless knowledge and limitless growth, does not belong to human beings. The subsequent collapse of innovation and creativity in the world of Islam was connected to the abandonment of the underpinnings of the traditional worldview which is based on unity (tawheed).*

COMMUNITIES AND CITIES AS INNOVATION LABS

Key enablers for innovation include an ecosystem for idea generation, incubation and diffusion. Cities and communities are living labs for innovation, seeking inspiration from the first city that the Prophet Mohammad (peace be upon him) founded in Medina and the social contract that embodies reason, diversity, social cohesion and ethics. In the twenty-first century rebuilding the cities in MENA will offer an opportunity for establishing a model of creative and innovative cities.

Can we envision Mecca and Medina as smart, green cities, demonstrating a global model on the innovation-sustainability nexus?

The focus of Islamic civilization has always been the *city* – the *medina*, from which the Arab word *tamaddun* (civilization) derives. The old Islamic cities underwent many cycles of rise and fall during waves of colonialism. This resulted in the decline of innovative cities which are the habitat and open laboratories for innovation. The city is increasingly conceptualized using terms such as "creative city" (Landry, 2008) which stresses the importance of culture and the arts in the urban context. The urban environment is an incubator for innovative ideas. The city is a barometer and an indicator of the level of urban innovation and the good life as reflected in a new index, i.e., the "urban innovation matrix".

In sum, it is imperative to develop a *culture for integral innovation* in the developing world through a purposeful reform of educational, STI and development policies. What is needed in the twenty-first century is development of a critical mass of scientists and researchers in the developing and developed world who can work on joint R&D, long term, collaborative projects to leapfrog to innovative technologies and rebuild innovative cities. This requires an enabling environment, an ecosystem for innovation and linkage to markets and industries. It is crucial that STI is mainstreamed, defined and framed as an integral part of national development strategies in the Arab region. In addition, it is vital to develop and provide evidence for a culture of innovation that can harness and unlock the best human capital. Rooting innovation and R&D culture in the local context and forging a new social contract between science and society are critical to the rebirth of an innovative ICON.

References and related bibliography

Adams, W. M., and Jeanrenaud, S. (2008). *Transition to Sustainability: Towards a Humane and Diverse World*. Gland: IUCN.

ADB, UNEP and UNESCAP. (2012) *Green Growth, Resources and Resilience: Environmental Sustainability in Asia and the Pacific*. Available online at http://www.unescap.org/resources/green-growth-resources-and-resilience-environmental-sustainability-asia-and-pacific [Accessed August 2015].

Ahmad, I. (1992). *The Rise and Decline of Muslim Ummah*. New Delhi: Adam Publishers.

Al-Faruqi, R. I. and Nasseef, O. A. (eds). (1981) *Social and Natural Sciences: The Islamic Perspective*. Jeddah: Hodder and Stoughton.

Al-Jabri, M. A. (2011). *Formation of Arab Reason: Text, Tradition and the Construction of Modernity in the Arab World* (Vol. 5). London: IB Tauris.

Al-Jayyousi, O. R. (2016). *Islam and Sustainable Development: New Worldviews.* Abingdon: Routledge.

Allawi, A. A. (2009). *The Crisis of Islamic Civilization.* New Haven, CT: Yale University Press.

Anawati, C. G. (1976) The significance of Islam's scientific heritage for the Moslem world today. *Impact of Science on Society,* 26(3), 161–167.

Arrow, K. (1962). Economic welfare and the allocation of resources for invention. In: R. Nelson (ed.) *The Rate and Direction of Inventive Activity: Economic and Social Factors.* Princeton, NJ: Princeton University Press (pp. 609–626).

Badawi, J. A. (2002) Islamic worldview: prime motive for development. *Humanomics,* 18(3/4), 325.

Bausani, A. (1974). Islam as an essential part of western culture. In: *Studies on Islam: A Symposium on Islamic Studies Organized in Cooperation with the Accademia dei Lincei in Rome.* Amsterdam and London: North-Holland Publishing Company, pp. 19–36.

Bennabi, M. (1988) *Islam in History and Society.* Islamabad: Islamic Research Institute.

Capra, F. (1983). *The Turning Point: Science, Society, and the Rising Culture.* New York: Bantam.

Freeman, C. (1982). The economics of industrial innovation. *University of Illinois at Urbana-Champaign's Academy for Entrepreneurial Leadership Historical Research Reference in Entrepreneurship.* Available online at http://ssrn.com/abstract=1496190 [Accessed August 2015].

Freeman, C. and Soete, L. (1997). *The Economics of Industrial Innovation.* New York: Psychology Press.

Freeman, C., Clark, J. and Soete, L. (1982). *Unemployment and Technical Innovation: A Study of Long Waves and Economic Development.* London: Burns & Oates.

Guessoum, N. (2012). Issues and agendas of Islam and science. *Zygon®,* 47(2), 367–387.

Hawken, P., Lovins, A. B. and Lovins, L. H. (2013). *Natural Capitalism: The Next Industrial Revolution.* London: Routledge.

Hillenbrand, C. (2000). *The Crusades: Islamic Perspectives.* Hove: Psychology Press.

Howard, D. (2014) *Being Human in Islam.* London: Routledge.

Iqbal, M. (1986) *The Reconstruction of Religious Thought in Islam.* Iqbal Academy Pakistan: Institute of Islamic Culture.

Kazzi, H. (2014). Green growth and sustainable development in the Arab countries. *European Scientific Journal,* 10(14).

Landry, C. (2008). The creative city: its origins and futures. *Urban Design-New Series,* 106, 14.

Lessem, R. and Schieffer, A. (2008). *Integral Research: A Global Approach towards Social Science Research Leading to Social Innovation.* Germany: BoD–Books on Demand.

Lessem, R. and Schieffer, A. (2016). *Integral research and Innovation: Transforming Enterprise and Society.* Boca Raton, FL: CRC Press.

Lovins, A. B., Lovins, L. H. and Hawken, P. (1999). *A Road Map for Natural Capitalism.* *Harvard Business Review*, 77(3), 145–158.

Lundvall, B. Å. (1988). Innovation as an interactive process. In: Dosi, G., Freeman, C., Nelson, R., Silverberg, O. and Soete, L. *Technical Change and Economic Theory.* London: Pinter Publishers, pp 349–369.

Lundvall, B. A. (1992). National Systems of Innovation: An Analytical Framework. London: Pinter.

Morrow, K. (2012). Rio+ 20, the green economy and re-orienting sustainable development. *Environmental Law Review*, 14(4), 279–297.

Nasr, S. (2003) *Science and Civilization in Islam.* Cambridge: Islamic Texts Society.

Nelson, R. L. (1959). Merger movements and business cycles, 1895–1956. In: *Merger Movements in American Industry, 1895–1956*. Princeton, NJ: Princeton University Press, (pp. 106–126).

Nelson, R. (1962). The link between science and invention: The case of the transistor. In: *The Rate and Direction of Inventive Activity: Economic and Social Factors.* Princeton, NJ: Princeton University Press, (pp. 549–584).

Nelson, R. (ed.) (1993) *National Innovation Systems: A Comparative Analysis.* New York and London: Oxford University Press.

Rushd, I. (1954). *Averroes' Tahafut Al-Tahafut: The Incoherence of the Incoherence.* London: Luzac.

Sabra, A. I. (1987). The Appropriation and subsequent naturalization of Greek science in medieval Islam: a preliminary statement. *History of Science*, 25, 223–243.

Saliba, G. (1999). *Rethinking the Roots of Modern Science:* Arabic Manuscripts in European Libraries. Washington, DC: Center for Contemporary Arab Studies (Georgetown University), Occasional Paper.

Saliba, G. (2000). Arabic versus Greek astronomy: A debate over the foundations of science. *Perspectives on Science*, 8(4), 328–341.

Saliba, G. (2002). Greek astronomy and the medieval Arabic tradition. The medieval Islamic astronomers were not merely translators. They may also have played a key role in the Copernican revolution. *American Scientist*, 90(4), 360–367.

Shlain, L. (1991) *Art and Physics, Parallel Visions in Space, Time and Light*, Quill Ed., New York: William Morrow Publishers.

Strange, T. and Bayley, A. (2008). *Sustainable Development: Linking Economy, Society, Environment, OECD Insights*, Paris: OECD Publishing.

Turner, R. H. (1995) *Science in Medieval Islam: An Illustrated Introduction.* Austin, TX: University of Texas Press.

2

Cultural innovation

2.1 Overview

Innovation can be informed not only by markets, but also by culture and the national vision. This chapter intends to shed some light on the influence of culture in shaping and framing the innovation canvas and agenda. The emergence of innovative nations may be viewed as a path-dependent trajectory. However, defining the key determinants and features of an innovative nation would provide useful insights. Key features for resilient and sustainable nations or organizations include openness to new ideas, responsiveness, flexibility and adaptation. This chapter attempts to address the conditions for renewal of a civilization since the sustainability-innovation nexus is underpinned by natural, social and intellectual capitals (see Figure 2.1). The ability to revive a nation is a rational and social choice that is framed, informed and reformed by culture.

The objectives of this chapter are outlined as follows:

- Introduce the roots of socio-technological innovation;

- Illustrate the linkages between society, culture and innovation;

- Propose a model for instilling a culture of innovation within organizations and societies;

- Consider new models of social innovation in the twenty-first century.

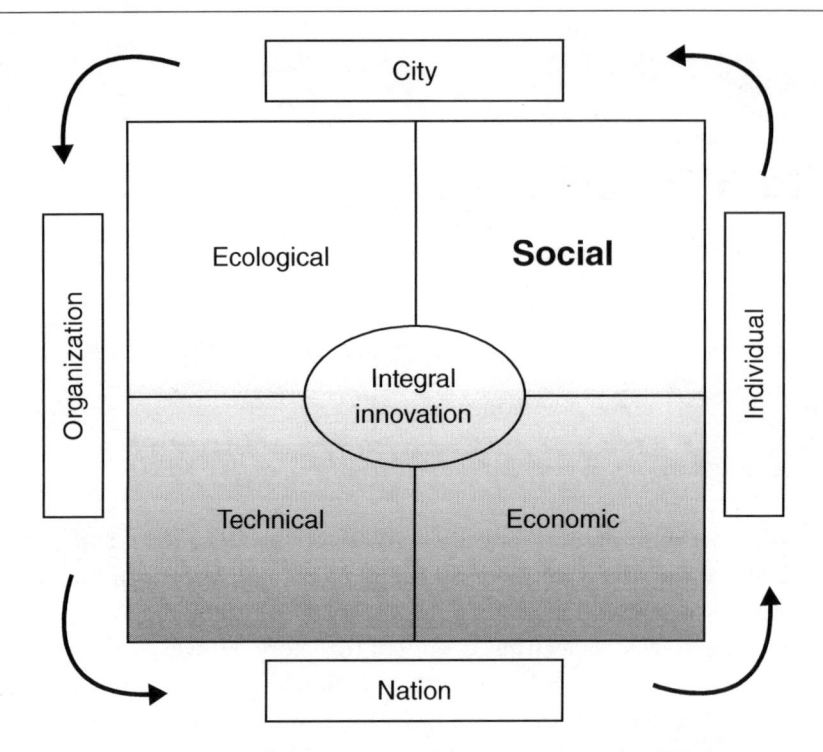

Figure 2.1   **A model for integral innovation focusing on social dimension**

2.2 Rise and fall of nations and organizations

The root of human innovation is inspired and informed by culture. The cycles of the rise and fall of nations are analogous to the natural cycles of water, carbon and nitrogen, and the business cycles. In this section, an attempt will be made to explain the role of culture in the evolution of the innovation-sustainability nexus. This chapter is intended to look at the cycles of rise and fall of nations so as to move beyond observation to realization and transformation. Also, it aims to shed light on the push and pull forces of mindsets and worldviews through history that were conducive to innovation in the national domain.

Can we co-create an innovative nation, society and organization? This question requires that we have a state of clarity on the key characteristics of an innovative nation. Mehdi Mozaffari (1998) argued that civilizations are formed as a result of a fusion of ideology and a historical system which is informed by a socio-political and economic system. Hence, to understand and instil innovation in a certain culture, it is essential to define the core elements and conditions that lock and unlock human potential and the collective ingredients of innovation and progress in ICONs.

The rise of ICONs is a path-dependent trajectory. Hence, it is insightful to characterize the key determinants for an innovative nation. Many civilizations have declined and ultimately died but they may still have the social DNA for renewal. Seeking inspiration from the past (or the Golden Age syndrome) may represent a driving force for many nations to overcome the hard realities of the present. Key features for resilient and sustainable nations or organizations include openness to new ideas, responsiveness, flexibility and adaptation.

The transformational journey to progress entails mastering of the art of "swimming upstream" to overcome challenges and conflicts within and between civilizations. The key challenge, I think, is to resolve the conflicts and dichotomies within a civilization, as in the case in the Islamic civilization. One of the key questions to be addressed is: Can a declined civilization re-emerge as a new, reformed civilization?

The theories about the cycles of civilization as articulated by Ibn Khaldun stipulate that there is an ecological or biological process that each civilization passes through. The collapse of early civilizations was attributed to scarcity of, or lack of access to, natural resources, extreme climate conditions, poor governance and social injustice. Hence, one may argue that the sustainability-innovation nexus is underpinned by natural, social, technological (or manufactured) and intellectual capitals. The ability to invent and innovate is critical for sustaining a nation or organization.

History, economics, ecology and culture shape our mental models of various forms of innovation. In the MENA region, it is illuminating to know that spirituality is a source of inspiration for cultural innovation, eco-innovation and naturalistic and eco-cosmic intelligence. This was manifested in narratives in the Quran about learning from species, ecology and metaphors inspired from all communities of life. In essence, studying nature as signs from the Creator framed and defined the Islamic meta-narrative about the role of man as a trustee and witness to protect the natural balance and embody inner change. This notion was emphasized by Iqbal (1986, p. 10) in a reflection on the Quranic verse: "Verily God will not change the condition of people, till they change what is in themselves" (Quran, 13: 11).

The metaphors, analogies and images in the Quran nurture the mind and spirit to form an enlightened society (Iqbal, 1986). The diversity of cultures, faiths and languages of Arabs, Persians, Turks, Africans and Indians contributed to the fusion of innovative ideas that produced new knowledge. In the field of medicine, Muslims translated the medical knowledge of the Greeks during the seventh and eighth centuries. The translation movement of the twelfth century in Latin Europe affected all fields of knowledge (Myers, 1964).

Islamic civilization offers a rich imagination for revival and reconstruction of an innovative nation. The narrative of past glory may help to instil a sense of optimism but should not be a panacea for complacency and overlooking rational imperatives. The following summarizes the key contributions of Islamic civilization in STI.

The work of the 1001 Inventions organization covering the Golden Age (Al-Hassani, 2012) reveals that there are missing links in terms of the intercultural fusion and proper documentation of the contribution of Islamic civilization in the West. This may explain partially the lack of proper understanding in Western culture of other cultures, and of Islam in particular. The Golden Age of Islamic Civilization, during the period that covered about 800 years (from the seventh to the fifteenth century) witnessed remarkable contributions in STI. Knowledge navigators and a community of practice in STI emerged which included Ibn Sina, Al-Khwarizmi and Al-Biruni who made contributions in both natural and physical sciences like biology, chemistry, physics, mathematics, medicine and astronomy. Hence, it is argued that the European Renaissance benefitted from the contribution of Muslim science during the Golden Age (Sarton, 1927, p. 17).

Two Muslim physicians who became well known in Europe during this period were Ibn Sina (980–1037) and Al-Razi (865–925). Ibn Sina devoted his life to the study of medicine, philosophy and other branches of science. Known in the West as Avicenna, Ibn Sina was a pioneer in discovering treatments for diseases using surgery and herbs. A key contribution to Islamic civilization was the development of the theory of numbers (*'ilm al-a'dad*) (Berggren, 1997). Moreover, in the tenth century, Mohammad Bin Ahmed, invented the concept of zero (Badawi, 2002). This was a breakthrough discovery which influenced all domains of science.

In addition, many Muslim thinkers contributed to maths and science. For example, Al-Khwarizmi was a pioneer in his writings in algebra in the twelfth century (Kettani, 1976). Umar Khayyam contributed to articulation of the cubic equations and Al-Battani contributed to trigonometry (Kettani, 1976). These discoveries led to advances in astronomy and geography. Also, Ibn al-Haytham (965–1041) made remarkable contributions in optics and theory of light (Myers, 1964, p. 32). Al-Haytham made contributions to geometry and number theory and studied the links between algebra and geometry (Myers, 1964).

Throughout the twelfth and thirteenth centuries in Spain and Sicily, the translation between Latin and the Arabic language enhanced knowledge sharing and cross-fertilization of ideas. The culture of co-existence and scientific inquiry in Sicily enabled cultural diversity and innovation (Crombie, 1963).

Reflecting on the drivers and enablers for an innovative culture, it can be seen that the resilience and sustainability of Islamic civilization was attributed to a number of factors. These include a shared consciousness for progress, multi-culturalism as a pre-condition for innovation, champions for change as catalysts for innovation and cross-fertilization on ideas as key enablers for innovation. These factors are discussed in turn.

SHARED CONSCIOUSNESS FOR PROGRESS

Nations are driven by a compelling and well-articulated vision about the future. The revival of many innovative regions like the USA and the EU, and organizations like 3M and P&G or individual leaders like Mandela or Ghandi was shaped by a vision and a dream. The literature on the reasons for the decline of nations is analogous to the natural law of decline as manifested in ecology, biology, economy and technology. Moreover, in theology it is illuminating to note that a state of decline is followed by an innovative era and a mandate to reconstruct and develop as reflected in the Book of Genesis and in Mesopotamian creation stories, the fall of human almost coincides with the making of the world (Fleischer, 1970, p. 1).

There are a number of approaches adopted to study and diagnose the decline of nations including the *biological-cyclical*, and the *structural*. The first one considers civilizations as similar to human biological life: birth, youth, adult, elderly and, finally, death. Also, Quigley sees civilizations moving through seven stages: 1) mixture, 2) gestation, 3) expansion, 4) conflict, 5) universal empire, 6) decay, and 7) invasion (Quigley, 1961).

However, there is a chance for renewal for a nation when it reaches a state of decay as argued by Arnold Toynbee who stated that there is a duality of "challenge-response" that maintains the dynamics of socio-political forces. The dual approach emphasizes the role of threat and conflict on the demise of nations, while the structuralism approach considers internal factors like socio-economics, infrastructure and commerce as key drivers for change. This social dynamic is described by Toynbee as a struggle between the nomadic or barbarian and civil nation-state models (Toynbee, 1995, p. 56). On the other hand, Ibn Khaldun attributed the decline of nations to the lack of social solidarity or social capital (*asabiyya*) and to injustice (poor governance) since the process of progress and construction (*Imran*) requires collective efforts (Ibn Khaldun, 1968, p. 103).

A shared consciousness for progress is manifested in a national agenda or vision for development which is fuelled by innovation. Nations are sustained when they master the art of harnessing innovation for development.

MULTI-CULTURALISM AS A PRE-CONDITION FOR INNOVATION

Diversity is vitality and a recipe for innovation and prosperity. Mono-cultures are less resilient and lack the energy for sustainable innovation. The sustainability of civilizations is underpinned by openness and the adoption of new ideas from other cultures. In the twenty-first century, we need to reconcile the value of multi-culturalism and multi-ethnicity for nurturing and enriching the sustainability-innovation nexus in an era of global change. In an era that is characterized by instability and the vulnerability of refugees, a new awareness of the value of human diversity and mobility needs to be reconstructed. I argue that vitality and innovation emanates from the unlocked potential of refugees moving across borders. This human capital is charged and able to make a difference due to their high drive for innovation, risk taking and entrepreneurship.

The renewal and revival of nations is viewed as part of either a corrective or progressive-cumulative process which is, in turn, part of the "challenge-response" process. As noted by Toynbee, a civilization which has been challenged is called to provide an adequate response. Its survival depends on the success of the response to risks and threats. He puts it in the following way: "Civilizations, I believe, come to birth and proceed to grow by successfully responding to successive challenges, they break down and go to pieces if and when a challenge confronts them which they fail to meet." (Toynbee, 1948, p. 56)

Hence, the bounded instability that may result from potential risks like refugees may be a source for social renewal. Multi-culturalism is a recipe for cross-fertilization which produces a fertile soil for innovation. This fusion of ideas and approaches from other cultures is likely to play a catalytic role in reinventing and inspiring new models for social transformation. Any nation, organization or individual who cannot master the art of celebrating diversity will have limited opportunities for renewal and sustainable innovation.

CHAMPIONS FOR CHANGE AS CATALYSTS FOR INNOVATION

Human capital is a key driver for cultural innovation. Champions and change agents play a critical role in inspiring communities, organizations and nations. Leadership is the cornerstone for instilling a culture and climate of innovation. An innovative nation is fuelled by challenges and its resilience depends on the leadership role taken in transforming challenges to opportunities. However, individuals need to form an ecosystem for innovation and to establish communities of practice to co-create new knowledge and a culture and climate for innovation. It is illuminating to reflect on the views of Ibn Khaldun with respect to the renewal or recovery of nations where he argues that the recovery of a declined civilization or nation hinges on enlightened individuals and the collective sense of shared destiny or social solidarity (*asabiyya*).

Organic and transformational leadership that is rooted in the local context and combines local identity and global integrity is crucial for shaping an innovative nation. Mahatir Mohammad of Malaysia is a good example of an innovative leader.

CROSS-FERTILIZATION ON IDEAS AS KEY ENABLERS FOR INNOVATION

The revival of a nation implies having a new social DNA and positive energy that is able to reconstruct a new model of human emancipation at all levels. In essence, nations pass through the fusion and convergence of ideas through a cross-fertilization of cultures. This process may entail either disintegration of one culture or the replacement by another as part of the natural cycle of the rise and fall of nations (Fukuyama, 1992).

In the twenty-first century, Western civilization may be viewed to be at a crossroads; the choice being either to pass through a decline and decay stage or to revive and reverse the decline as argued by Huntington (1996). The alternative approach to the cyclical one is the progressive-cumulative approach which is based on the belief of the cumulative character of human experiences. Kant, as a founder of the progressive-cumulative school of thought, views a dynamic social process which is characterized by the successive destruction of civilizations, where each culture maintains and/or gets rid of some of its past ingredients to move forwards to a new "innovative field". This cycle of decay-renewal can be seen in the succession of Greek, Roman, Islamic and Western civilizations.

The innovative power of nations is a journey from a resource-based economy to a knowledge economy to a new consciousness. This notion was documented by Hegel when he defined the goal of history as follows: "the History of the world is none other than the progress of consciousness of Freedom" (Hegel, 1953).

In the twenty-first century, as we are faced with global challenges from poverty to climate change, the idea of progress is interlinked with the innovation-sustainability nexus. This in turn explains that the natural cycle of the rise and fall of nations is crucial for evolving a new consciousness and redefining a new agenda for a sustainable human civilization. From an Islamic perspective, the purpose and mandate of human civilization is to construct and develop this planet. The following section outlines the key features for an innovative nation from an Islamic perspective.

2.3 Innovation in the Islamic civilization

Islamic civilization is part of the historical continuum and human history from all prophets including Abraham, Moses and Jesus. The core is the same: all humans have the same origin and will face the same destiny and their value is judged by good performance. The discourse that informs a universal model for an innovative community and city was contextualized in the city of Medina as founded by Prophet Mohammad (peace be upon him). The initiation of an innovative community/city in Medina was based on the following key components:

- Innovative individuals who migrated from their home land, i.e., refugees (*muhajerin*) who moved from Mecca to Medina;

- A new brand and name for the city (urban space) from "*yathrib*" to "*madina*"; a term that is linked to civilization (*tamaddun*) which means a new civil public domain and public space;

- A constitution that had a unifying social contract, mandate and vision for the community;

- The cultural diversity of the community which consisted of people from Persia, Central Asia, Africa and Arabia;

- An integrative and dynamic strategy of communication with neighbouring nations to reach a common articulation and agreement on global commons like human dignity, peace and freedom.

The ninth century (AD) witnessed a rise of intellectual and institutional innovation during the reign of Al-Ma'mûn (813–833) who established Bayt al-Hikma (the House of Wisdom). This era of enlightenment continued until the thirteenth century when philosophy and religion were considered two distinct domains of knowledge as articulated by Al-Fârâbi (827–950) (Kraemer, 1986, p. 15). This era was characterized by universal values and openness to other cultures. Later, this vibrant civilization declined which raises the question of why this occurred. One explanation attributes this to the fact that philosophy was more textual than critical. Another explanation states that this was due to the fact that Arab philosophers did not reconcile the two domains of knowledge, revelation and philosophy, and, hence, there was limited adoption of rationalism in science and technology, which was adopted in Western culture. The renaissance of rationalism in Western civilization was characterized by three elements: 1) the pursuit of mathematical reasoning, 2) the transfer of science to technology, and 3) the development of an institutional setup in organizations

(Shayegan, 1997, p. 85). These key enablers of renaissance and rationalism in Western culture enabled a process of reformation and reconstruction.

In essence, the Renaissance was based on reconstruction of the Greek and Roman cultures which was a fusion of the world of ideas and the world of things, referred to as the Western reconnaissance model. Muslim thinkers and reformers like Al-Afghani and Mohamad Abdoh were influenced by the Western model and articulated a new discourse to reproduce, revive and innovate Islamic culture based on the Medina model. As argued by Nasr (1996), harnessing Western science and technology is instrumental for modernization (*tajdid*). The key features for the Medina model are summarized below:

- *A value-based society*: The Medina model was informed by a global vision and philosophy. It is simply a pilot civic initiative to move from a nomadic culture to a formal urban culture based on cooperation, sharing of resources and respect for rights.

- *Collective responsibility*: The Medina model was innovative in forming a collective model for social responsibility and sharing of resources. At its core are ethical values, balanced with economic rationality.

- *Co-existence*: The core of a civic life and urban culture is diversity and co-existence. An ethical code of conduct organized the relationships of a value-based and multi-cultural community.

- *Innovation*: The idea of a distinction between sacred and practical knowledge was made clear by the incident of the palm trees and the Prophet ruling "you know better in your daily business affairs". This is a clear message and mandate to pursue intellect and experience in solving current issues outside the realm of spirituality.

- *A new consciousness*: The realization and awareness of other cultures and the respect for common values were clear in the charter of Medina which is about defending global common interests and human values.

- *Entrepreneurship and social innovation*: The openness for initiative in social responsibility and social innovations was clear in the case of Abdul Rahman ibn Awf, a good example of an entrepreneur who succeeded in creating wealth. The innovation in the Medina model is illustrated in the development of a holistic worldview that encompasses social, economic and human transformation. Revival was rooted in local knowledge used to establish a new value-based society founded on reason, empathy and faith. Social innovation through the establishing and redefining of public goods like a trust fund for water (*Waqf*) and protected areas for grazing (the *Hima* system) represented a form of integral innovation at the level of an "idea-organization-society".

Cultural innovation and the revival of a nation embody two components: having a *universal vision* and a *historical memory of achievement*. The two parts constitute a combination of the past (historical memory) and future (universal vision). An innovative nation is measured by its capacity to reconcile, adapt and frame a unifying narrative that is inspired by the past and driven by the future. Western civilization was driven and guided by a number of rational imperatives which included technological rationality nurtured by scientific inquiry and freedom. In essence, the reconstruction of a declined civilization is realized through a process of collective social learning and reflection. The reconstruction of a global Muslim civilization can be founded on global norms based on human rights, co-existence, freedom, equity and ethics. For nations in transition, an articulation of both global vision and legacy is necessary to establish a new narrative for a global civilization which is informed by a dynamic process of response and challenge.

An innovative reconstruction of an Islamic civilization implies a deep understanding and realization that is likely to entail new modalities and models of governance and business models that respond to real-world challenges and constraints. In sum, a cultural/ social innovation entails a narrative on what constitutes a model of an innovative culture. The Medina model, which was established during the Prophet's time, represents a holistic approach for celebrating unity within diversity. Reform and enlightenment attempts in the Middle East were underpinned by social justice and freedom. The pursuit of cultural innovation from an Islamic perspective represents a renewal and a reformation process that is informed by global experiences.

In today's global crises, which include human health, poverty, finance and ecology, Islam can offer a fresh and renewed model for a redefinition of the progress of societies. This is attained through an articulation of what constitutes a good life (*hayat tayebeh*) and is also part of a larger process of civic renewal (Al-Jayyousi, 2016). It is enlightening to realize the historical role of the Islamic culture and worldviews in promoting co-existence, socialization of knowledge and dialogue between cultures. Ibn Khaldun in his *Mukadimmah* (1968) presented a social theory for explaining the rise and fall of nations during the Muslim rule in Spain and North Africa. He developed a theory of economic cycles which is an inter-temporal analysis of socio-economic and political changes. He also outlined the societal transformation from nomadic (*badawah*) to urban (*madaneyah*). Ibn Khaldun (1968) argued that "it is the sociological make-up of society which holds the secret to economic growth and decline".

An understanding of the interaction between demographic, technological and institutional factors would provide fundamental insights into societal transformation and renewal. Also of special significance is the notion of *Assabiyah* (group solidarity, group consciousness) that Ibn Khaldun (1968) introduced to explain social cohesion. *Assabiyah* is a group feeling and energy that emerges from the unity of social, economic and political interests. The existing social solidarity is conducive to the provision of economic activities that, in turn, provide further impetus for social solidarity.

In sum, cultural values shape and inform a climate and an enabling environment for innovation. Technology and values interact to influence social choices for innovation and development. The following section outlines the role of cultural values and technology in development.

2.4 Cultural values and technology

Human worldviews are shaped and influenced by ecology, culture and technology. This, in turn, frames a group of mindsets including environmental, cultural and technological determinism. While environmental determinism informs a compelling paradigm in development, education and policy, *cultural determinism* defines the driving forces for community action and choice. On the other hand, *technological determinism* assumes that technological innovation drives social transformation and change.

It is argued that values and culture influence technology selection and innovation culture. Modern technology is seen as essentially alien to traditional cultural systems, intruding into local cultures, thus cutting off the potential for developing traditional and local technologies. There is a sense of scepticism regarding the social impact of technological innovations, in terms of social cohesion and employment. There is a typical social sentiment of longing and appreciating the past which is referred to as the Golden Age syndrome (Moore, 1980).

Technology is shaping human behaviour as illustrated by the use of public transport influencing traveller behaviours and land use patterns. Recent innovative technologies in media, education, business, information and telecommunications, energy, water, and food have transformed people's values, habits and business operations in banking, education, business and trade. Moreover, market globalization has changed the perception of time and space and introduced the notion of the global village. The web-based social media has led to the development of new modes of open and user innovation, crowdsourcing and crowdfunding.

Public policy and government play a key role in technology acquisition and selection. Technology choice can shape the trajectory for sustainable development as manifested in mega-projects in infrastructure, water, energy, agriculture and transport. However, the trade-offs and/or combination of market-oriented and public policies are debated in many developing countries concerning their adequacy for achieving social justice and equity considering the digital divide between the haves and the have nots. In many cases, decisions for technology adoption (as in the case of nuclear energy or public transport) are influenced by political power and the technical and professional advice is marginalized.

The adoption of green energy technologies, or nuclear energy, is a good example of the divergence in values within society. Values intervene in the process of examining possible technological alternatives as in the case of the construction of water dams, waste disposal, alternative energy or public transit technology. The debate is linked to social values and technology policy as illustrated in the case of the importation of *capital-intensive technologies* versus *labour-intensive technologies;* which is simply a debate about *efficiency versus equity.*

Another domain of cultural innovation may include models of social innovation which may be viewed as a response from people acting to support their values or protect public goods and global commons in all fields of life from education, environment, gender, human rights and public affairs as illustrated in the following case study on the We Love Reading social enterprise in Jordan founded by Dr Rana Dajani.

In sum, instilling a culture of innovation is critical to embedding technology in a nation but it is more important to realize that innovation inspired from culture is the cornerstone for harnessing technology as a means to emancipation and freedom. The key challenge for many developing countries is to define a path and a plan for cultural innovation. Reviving a declined culture requires a collective effort and integral innovation at all levels and domains.

2.5 Case study 2.1: Social innovation by Dr Rana Dajani, Jordan

When one changes communities and living spaces one sees things in a different way. This is what happened to me. Coming back to Jordan after having spent five years aboard I saw the country with a different eye: things I had taken for granted, things I had not noticed, things I had accepted that were wrong but did nothing about because I thought it was beyond my capabilities.

I realized that children were not reading for pleasure. They read for education and religion but not for pleasure, although reading for pleasure is very important because reading is essential to the development of children's personalities,

> ### We Love Reading and social entrepreneurship – Dr Rana Dajani
>
> We are born as children into our families and communities. We go about life interacting with the other humans in our circle. Through these interactions we develop our personalities and who we are, as well as our values and morals. We come to realize that there are some things around us that are not right and seem to be against what we have grown up to think is right and just. We question and object but we are told that is how things are and we cannot change them because such change requires something greater than the individual. Or that it is the responsibility of the people in power, the government. As humans we all have the ability to identify problems and challenges but few are those who actually go beyond and create solutions. By creating solutions, one becomes a social entrepreneur. I believe we all have it in us to be social entrepreneurs. We just have to discover our inner potential to unleash our creativity to make a change, however small, within our circles. Many have already started. For some it is obvious, for others it is not so obvious but it is there creating small ripples of change the consequence of which may not be felt until generations to come.
>
> I grew up in a family that valued time and education. We were always questioned by my parents on what we had been doing with our time. Had it been spent doing something useful for ourselves or the community around us? We were also instilled with a feeling of responsibility towards the community; that as Muslims we shoulder the problems and should seek to create solutions: "everyone is a guardian" and that is the purpose of our lives.
>
> We were also taught that Allah would not judge us on the results but only on our intentions and efforts because the results are not in our hands. These three values inspired me later on to develop We Love Reading.

imagination and cognitive skills. This lack of reading was not only exhibited in Jordan but across the Arab world and in developing countries.

As a scientist, I was curious to find out why. I did my own research and discovered that the reason children do not read for pleasure is because they do not love to read. In order to make children love to read they have to be read to from an early age, even as early as when the mother is pregnant so that a feeling of security and happiness is connected to reading that stays with the child forever, so that he/she resorts to reading whenever they feel happy or sad because it gives them a good feeling reminiscent of their childhood.

At this point I realized that I knew the solution to making children love to read. Parents should read aloud to their children. However, it is impossible to train every parent to read aloud. The alterative would be to pass a law that parents should read aloud but even if I convinced someone in the government to pass such a law, this would not guarantee that parents would read aloud to their children. Therefore, I thought that there was nothing I could do at this point. The solution was beyond my control. As most people do, I would just carry on my life as usual, content that I had tried.

However, I was brought up on the values that we are responsible for the community and knowledge is a responsibility that should be passed on. I therefore felt that I had to do something with this knowledge of mine. I felt that I was responsible for all the children in my community not reading because I had a solution. Reading to my children was not enough. My responsibility extended beyond my little circle… to the wider community.

So, I decided I would start reading aloud to the children in my community. I would be the change. Ghandi said, "be the change you want to see in the world", and there is a verse in the Quran stating that, "you have to change yourself". This is the first step in social entrepreneurship. The resolution to take action as an individual is critical for the journey of discovery.

I gathered my family and explained to them what I was planning to do. I asked for their advice and support and contributions to be part of the team. They were all excited and on board with ideas and suggestions. We wanted to read aloud to the children in the neighbourhood. We needed a space to do so. We looked around us and asked where there was a good place that was appropriate for children, safe, clean, with a bathroom, etc. and we also asked ourselves whether we could find a space where we could read aloud in every neighbourhood. In Jordan there is a mosque in every neighbourhood. So we thought why not use the mosque. It fitted all the criteria for reading aloud to children. Involving the family is very important. No one works in isolation. Team work is essential. Involving the family is even more relevant as a social entrepreneur to rally all members of society to work together for the greater good. This also allows for drawing upon the experience and wisdom of community members. They become your champions when the going is rough and support you throughout. In this way you also become a role model for the new generation and give them a chance to be part of something bigger.

So, my husband went to the person in charge of the mosque and explained to him that I was going to read aloud to the children. Since I am a member of the neighbourhood and he knows me and my family I was welcome to read in the mosque. I am not someone from outside the community so my intentions were not in question. The imam suggested announcing the reading-aloud programme during the Friday prayer session to invite children to attend. We decided to hold the reading-aloud session on Saturday mornings. A very important aspect of our model is that we do not create new centres but utilize existing locations (the mosques) as vehicles for the delivery of our innovation. The We Love Reading (WLR) model opens mosques to children and allows women to have a leadership role within their spaces. Mosques are also the cornerstones of WLR sustainability, since they are in every neighbourhood and are accessible to all. The mosques are crucial to the sustainability and replicability of our model and are essential to community involvement.

The children's ages ranged from four to ten. I chose this age range because the younger children are the easier it is to instil a love of reading. But I could not include children who were too young otherwise I would have to convince the parents to come. It is easier to change children than adults. I also did not choose to include children older than ten because it is more difficult to instil the love of reading in older children and they would require a different genre of books.

The books I chose to read to the children were age appropriate, in the native language, colourful and attractive. The content of the books was neutral, not related to any religion or ideology. The children initially came to the read aloud session because their parents forced them to. However, after listening to the stories being read aloud to them in an animated way, they fell in love and demanded to come every Saturday morning.

The idea was that the children would become the proponents for reading in their homes and communities rather than being the respondents. This created children who do things for their own good not because someone has told them to do something. This is how we begin to create change makers within society. The children become readers for life. The programme creates a lifelong enthusiasm for each child to read and acquire knowledge, particularly benefitting girls, ensuring their ability to build better social and economic living conditions and improve their wellbeing.

The model gradually developed over the years in a kind of human-centred design; trying out different modalities to figure out what works and what does not. It was very important to define the most cost efficient and effective model to achieve the goal intended. Currently the model consists of a volunteer adult from the community, who does not have to be highly educated, who reads aloud to children in a public space on a routine basis. The model is very simple. Anyone can start anywhere. The model is very flexible. Every woman who adopts it tailors it to fit her community, schedule, culture and needs. This aids in building her ownership of the project and therefore its sustainability, because she becomes a partner in the development of the model.

The volunteer adult gets the incentive from the community because the parents appreciate what the volunteer has done for their children. The volunteer becomes a kind of leader in the community. Members of the community start donating books or money to buy books. In this way the model is sustainable and builds ownership in the volunteer reader and members of the community. This buy in from the community is a very important aspect of successful entrepreneurship.

Sustainability is built into our model through capacity building at the level of the local citizen. By providing programme development training to local women and girls we are instilling in them the confidence and skills they need to successfully expand WLR into their neighbourhoods with minimal guidance and resources. The women who receive training are required to "pay it forwards", by sharing their newly acquired knowledge and training another woman to become a reader and community leader. This creates a domino effect which means that the impact of the programme increases logarithmically.

Rather than importing solutions from outside the culture/country we should develop our own solutions. Such solutions are sustainable, more effective and create changemakers and leaders rather than victims and followers with no identity. International aid and development programmes should rethink how they support and help developing countries. It should allow the people to take charge and ask them how to help. A solution in one culture may not necessarily work in another. But more importantly it is essential that the people being helped have agency and ownership otherwise the victim attitude and dependency on others is propagated. Such attitudes and approaches do not build a nation or community, nor do they develop identity.

A successful social entrepreneur comes up with a solution that is simple, does not cost much and is sustainable. While we are used to a West to East flow of ideas and innovations, WLR is an example of an East to West flow. WLR has spread to Germany, Mexico and the USA. In addition to being implemented in Uganda, Malaysia, Azerbaijan and Turkey. Today more than ever, we are in need of home-grown role models to boost the confidence and preserve the identity of our youth; to aid them in defining who they are in a world that is becoming one global village; to make them aware that we can learn from others while maintaining our pride in our culture and heritage. Not all solutions are applicable across cultures and they should understand that every culture has something to give.

The WLR programme developed a training scheme to create WLR libraries in Jordan and all over the world. I created an NGO to be a legal umbrella for the programme. Many ideas do not get to the legal stage. This extra step needs support from a donor or sponsor. Therefore, we call upon donors and sponsors to search for these social entrepreneurs because their grassroots and home-grown solutions will eventually succeed. NGOs that have started otherwise usually do not succeed because there is no core around which the NGO was built.

Many of the women and men we have trained have become entrepreneurs themselves in projects beyond the WLR library. The function of creating WLR served as a stepping stone for them to discover their inner potential and to realize that they could achieve things on their own. That is all we need to become change makers. We need a testimonial to free us from all inhibitions and misconceptions whether internally or externally. That is what WLR does. This has succeeded with women and young men, housewives and grandparents. The added value is that WLR does so in a culturally sensitive way. As Kurt Hahn once said, "There is more in you than you think". Husbands and mosque clerics have all been supportive and encouraging of women holding read aloud sessions.

Almost all projects in the Arab world focus on innovation in the physical aspects of problems, rather than on the actual experience, while in the West the focus is on the experience. Hence grants are about buying equipment in the East, while in the West they are about building capacity because when you build an individual you are investing in the future; the individual can change the world and can affect others. A physical item is obsolete and does not make change by itself. Our innovation is in providing an experience rather than a physical thing. This is what is unique and innovative and creative in the WLR initiative. It is one of the rare initiatives that focus on the experience and building capacity rather than distributing reading material. This is not to belittle the need for the availability of reading materials, but that alone is not enough. Many people have huge libraries and do not read. When you love to read you will find books to read. Reading material is never the limiting factor.

All the projects in the Levant areas focus on providing books in different ways. But none to my knowledge focus on reading aloud. And if they do, it is as a by-product of the books' distribution or availability. In contrast, we have developed a model that provides a practical solution to solve the read aloud problem. In other words, our model is a substitute for the parent. We cannot train all parents to read aloud and to show passion for reading. But we can train one person per neighbourhood to do that and we have shown that this is enough. The next generation of children will grow up loving to read and they will become the parents of the future. The effect is logarithmic over generations in our theory of change. Our initiative has a long vision. We believe to initiate real change a project has to be from the grass roots and on a one-to-one basis, and it has to focus on experience and building human potential. Although this change is slow, it is real.

WLR has spread to 27 countries and has become a social movement. It combines five elements that are critical to achieving impact at scale:

1. We have developed a simple, effective product that appeals strongly to its market of mothers and children; a step by step guide to creating a read aloud group in a community. Our training method is simple, useful, repeatable and reliable.

2. WLR depends on networks. Many organizations both commercial and social mistake their own growth in sale revenues, profits or members for success. The bigger the organization gets the more successful it must be; WLR measures its success by how may children it gets involved in reading groups.

3. The women are becoming more than a network, they already resemble a movement to bring about social change through reading, albeit a movement that operates without attracting much attention, making much noise or seeking confrontation. WLR has the aim of bringing about long term cultural change. It is not delivering a service which needs a support system with a complex supply chain; it is creating capabilities in hundreds of local women enabling them to do something creative for themselves.

4. Organizations need hierarchies but movements need causes, shared values and common goals to pull them together and give them a purpose; reading is the means but the cause is to get children at a young age to realize they can and should think for themselves.

The model is formulated in such a way that each person can tailor the model to fit their culture and their needs while maintaining the essence of the model. WLR is spreading like wildfire in many countries.

The model also serves as a platform for dissemination of awareness programmes including hygiene and conservation of energy and water. It has been shown through research that it is the mother that plants these good habits at an early age in her child. Stories that she reads to the child can instil good habits of health and conserving the environment. The biggest problem facing most projects working on raising awareness in developing countries is accessing the grass roots. Our model does that. The second problem is trust, which our model provides by virtue of the locally administered library.

Scaling the concept of social entrepreneurship

To replicate the process of developing a solution at the individual level I have developed a programme at the university called the Community Awareness Programme. This stems from the belief that everyone is a social entrepreneur. They just do not know it. The aim of this project is the development of individuals to become responsible active participants in society. The project aims to develop confidence and leadership qualities in the students. These aspects are very important components of the student's university education. When students are exposed to the application of their knowledge they feel that they can make a difference and change the wrong things they see around them. This nurtures their feeling of responsibility towards the community and that they should do something. We have achieved these goals by teaching students to identify a problem in their environment, analyse the problem, create a plan to attempt to solve the problem and carry out the proposed plan. Students are required to keep a journal of the application of the plan which should include examples, narrations, good and bad experiences. At the end of the project students shared their experiences. This gave the students the chance to evaluate and criticize their plans after carrying them out.

The lessons learned from the analysis of social entrepreneurship allow us to start to define the essential ingredients of a robust national system of innovation (NIS) and innovation ecosystem and the best practices in harnessing innovation for development.

The objective of social entrepreneurship is to light a fire in the heart of every individual. In order to do that one must not underestimate the importance of the human interaction embodied in the inspiring persona of the teachers/role models and mentors. Everyone is special and it is imperative that the average individual succeeds. We are as strong as our weakest link. As the late King Hussein of Jordan said, the human being is the richest resource a nation can own. The individual must not disappear into the masses. Our focus on the individual will result in building confidence, resolution of the identity crisis and home-grown solutions. The individual must be supported in all modes of intelligence and in all disciplines not only the fields of science, technology, engineering and maths but also, most importantly, in the field of humanities. This should be achieved in addition to encouraging an evolution in our understanding of Islam to cope with modernity and globalization. In conclusion, in order for social entrepreneurship to succeed we must sustain an environment that supports freedom and demands responsibility that leads to accountability.

References and related bibliography

Abuja, R. (2004). "The Bridge-Builders": Some notes on railways, pilgrimage and the British "civilizing mission" in colonial India." In: *Colonialism as Civilizing Mission: Cultural Ideology in British India*, edited by H. Fischer-Tiné and M. Mann. London: Anthem Press,.

Agrawal, A. (1995). Dismantling the divide between indigenous and scientific knowledge. *Development and Change*, 26, 413–439.

Al-Hassani, S. T. (2012). *1001 Inventions: The Enduring Legacy of Muslim Civilization*. Washington, DC: National Geographic Books.

Al-Jayyousi, O. R. (2016). *Islam and Sustainable Development: New Worldviews*. London: Routledge.

Badawi, J. A. (2002). *Gender Equity in Islam* (Vol. 2, pp. 427–428). Indianapolis, IN: IDM Publications.

Berggren, J. L. (1997). Mathematics and her sisters in medieval Islam: A selective review of work done from 1985 to 1995. *Historia Mathematica*, 24(4), 407–440.

Beshore, G. (1998). *Science in Early Islamic Cultures*. New York: FranklinWatts.

Conklin, A. L. (1997). *A Mission to Civilize: The Republican Idea of Empire in France and West Africa. 1895-1930*. Stanford, CA: Stanford University Press.

Crombie, A. C. (1963). *Scientific Change: Historical Studies in the Intellectual, Social, and Technical Conditions for Scientific Discovery and Technical Invention, from Antiquity to the Present*. New York: Basic Books.

Diamond, J. (1997). *Guns, Germs and Steel: A Short History of Everybody for the Last 13,000 Years*. London: Jonathan Cape.

Faruqi, Y. M. (2006). Contributions of Islamic scholars to the scientific enterprise. *International Education Journal*, 7(4), 391–399.

Fleischer, H. (1970). *Marx Und Engels. Die Philosoph. Grundlinien Ihres Denkens.*, Freiburg/Munich: Alber.

Fukuyama, F. (1992). *The End of History and the Last Man*. New York: Penguin.

Headrick, D. R. (1981). *The Tools of Empire: Technology and European Imperialism in the Nineteenth Century*. New York: Oxford University Press.

Hegel, G. W. F. (1953). *Reason in History*. Trans. R. S. Hartman. New York: Macmillan Publishing Company.

Huntington, S. P. (1996). *The Clash of Civilizations and the Remaking of World Order*, New York: Simon & Schuster.

Ibn Khaldun, A. (1968), *The Muqaddimah*, trans. F. Rosenthal, 3 vols. London: Routledge & Kegan Paul.

Iqbal, A. M. (1986). *Reconstruction of Religious Thought in Islam*, edited and annotated by M. Saeed Sheikh, 2nd Edition. Lahore: Institute of Islamic Culture and Iqbal Academy Pakistan, p, 149.

Kettani, M. A. (1976). Moslem contributions to the natural sciences. *Impact of Science on Society*, 26(3), 135–147.

Kraemer, J. L. (1986). *Humanism in the Renaissance of Islam*, Leiden: E. J. Brill.

Landes, D. (1998). *The Wealth and Poverty of Nations: Why Some Are so Rich and Some so Poor*. New York: Norton.

Lemonnier, P. (ed.). (1993). *Technological Choices; Transformation in Material Cultures since the Neolithic.* London: Routledge.

Meri, J. W. (ed.). (2005). *Medieval Islamic Civilization: An Encyclopedia.* New York: Routledge.

Mitchell, T. (2002). *Rule of Experts: Egypt, Techno-Politics, Modernity.* Berkeley, CA: University of California Press.

Moore, S. W. (1980). *Marx on the Choice between Socialism and Communism.* Cambridge, MA: Harvard University Press.

Mozaffari, M. (1998). Can a declined civilization be reconstructed? *International Relations,* 14(3), 31–48.

Mozaffari, M. (2002). *Globalization and Civilizations.* Hove: Psychology Press.

Myers, E. A. (1964). *Arabic Thought and the Western World in the Golden Age of Islam.* New York: Ungar.

Nasr, S. V. r. (1996). *Mawardi and the Making of Islamic Revivalism.* New York: Oxford University Press.

Perkins, J. H. (1997). *Geopolitics and the green revolution: Wheat, genes, and the Cold War.* New York: Oxford University Press.

Quigley, C. (1961), *The Evolution of Civilizations: An Introduction to Historical Analysis,* New York: Macmillan.

Rashed, R. (2002). *Encyclopaedia of the History of Arabic Science.* London: Routledge.

Saliba, G. (2002). Greek astronomy and the medieval Arabic tradition. The medieval Islamic astronomers were not merely translators. They may also have played a key role in the Copernican revolution. *American Scientist,* 90(4), 360–367.

Sarton, G. (1927). *Introduction to the History of Science.* Baltimore, MD: Williams and Wilkins.

Shayegan, D. (1997). *Cultural Schizophrenia: Islamic Societies Confronting the West,* New York: Syracuse University Press.

Toynbee, A. (1995). *A Study of History,* London: Oxford University Press.

Walzer, R. (1985). (Translation and commentary by) *Al-Farabi on the Perfect State, Abu Nasr al-Farabi's Mabâdi' Arâ' Ahl-Al-Madîna Al-Fâdila,* Oxford: Clarendon Press.

3

Eco-innovation

3.1 Introduction

This chapter covers another dimension of integral innovation which is linked to nature, ecosystems or the environment as shown in Figure 3.1. Inspirations from nature can inform new sustainable business models which are referred to as eco-innovations. However, technology has created a gap and disconnection between humans and nature which is referred to as "human deficit disorder". There is a critical need to explain why biodiversity needs to be conserved and to define the value of nature for human inspiration, creativity and innovation. What we are witnessing in the state of the environment in terms of pollution, desertification, waste and species extinction is a symptom of an ethical and moral crisis. This requires an effort to translate faith into action to contribute to the human mission of construction of the Earth (*Emaratu Al-Ard*). Protecting this open source of innovation (as manifested in nature) is imperative for sustainable human civilization.

This chapter will focus on how innovation can be inspired by ecology and culture (Islam). The linkages between ecology and culture are evident in the rich use of metaphors and analogies in Islamic tradition. Both sources of knowledge in Islam, the Quran and Hadith, promote reflection on the cosmos, nature and human creation. Signs (*ayat*) of the Creator are evident in both the text (Quran) and in the creation of God in nature, the cosmos and humans. The following is a synthesis of the various dimensions and enablers that Islam utilized to inspire, inform and mainstream the principles of eco-innovations in the human mind. This chapter is based on my book titled *Islam and Sustainable Development: New Worldviews* (Al-Jayyousi, 2016).

The Islamic worldview sees unity and continuity in all religions and this unity transcends humans to include the cosmos and all living organisms around us. Living species are considered as "communities like humans" (*umam*; Sura 6:38). The inspiration for this holistic worldview is the notion that the whole of creation obeys natural laws and hence, in essence, every living organism is in a state of prayers

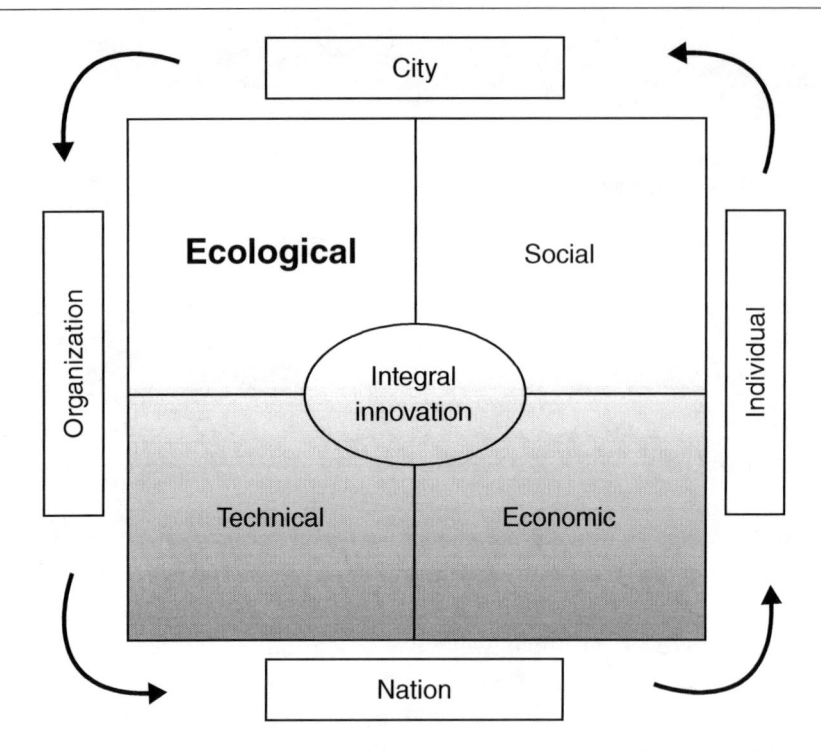

Figure 3.1   A model for integral innovation focusing on ecological dimension

(*tasbeeh* and *sujood*), which I call a symphony of life. Any human activity that causes harm to nature and life is disrupting this symphony. Another essential concept of the green movement in the Islamic worldview is that it is based on positive energy, hope and optimism. This was illustrated in the saying of Prophet Mohammad, "When doomsday comes, if someone has a palm shoot in his hand he should plant it". This is a vivid example of the imperative for the human role in making a difference through responsible action to save the planet and address ecological risks. In addition, Islamic discourse inspires imagination through guiding the human mind to reflect on the cycles of life and history and by using analogies and metaphors to illustrate notions of succession and innovation.

As articulated by Kiuchi and Shireman (2001), nature is a source of inspiration and imagination and it has been an R&D laboratory and open source for knowledge for more than 3.8 billion years. A key enabler for a transition to a knowledge economy is having the capacity to understand, learn and harness lessons embedded in nature. One key lesson to ensure sustainable innovation all levels (ICON) is to enhance the human capacity to learn from the creative systems of nature. Another key lesson from nature is to appreciate the value of diversity in sustaining the innovative capacity of organizations and nations since diversity brings vitality and resilience to the ecosystem of innovation. Societies and businesses may not only be *informed* by nature but may also be *reformed* by nature and culture. Valuing the hidden connections in nature (like the air, sun and nutrients in the soil) brings a deeper understanding of processes for innovation. This duality of the seen (*thaher*) and the unseen (*batin*) explains the essence of sustainable innovation.

The transition to green businesses and economies involves a lower ecological footprint, increased productivity and a reduction or elimination of waste. These conditions and constraints for eco-friendly businesses are drivers for eco-innovation. This in turn will drive our imaginations to mimic nature in sustaining life affirming and creative patterns of life through reducing and eliminating waste and instilling a new meaning of value that is not based on the acquisition of goods to but on simply accessing services.

3.2 The Islamic worldview on eco-innovation

Al-Jayyousi (2016) in *Islam and Sustainable Development* argued that eco-innovation concepts and metaphors are vividly described in Islamic thought. Islam teaches that species, both plants and wildlife, are in a state of *tasbeeh*. The harming of any species means disrupting the symphony of life and silencing worshippers. Quranic metaphors and analogies deepen the notion of ecological inspiration, aesthetic intelligence, biomimicry and learning from nature. Both the Quran and nature contain many signs that demonstrate and offer insights and guidance to nurture inspiration, naturalistic intelligence, innovation and learning. The notion of *ihsan* means inner beauty, continuous improvement and heightened consciousness. *Ihsan* is a key concept in Islam, being the driver and fuel for human stewardship, responsibility and excellence. *Zohd* (de-growth) means living lightly on the earth, which is an Islamic concept that promotes conservation and rational use of resources. Ghazi bin Mohammed, Reza Shah-Kazemi and Aftab Ahmed (2010) outlined the key elements of the environment in Islam as summarized in this section.

- *Creation is a reflection of Truth*: The created environment is not just a random form, but rather a reflection of the Truth.

- *Humans are responsible and accountable*: The notion that the natural environment is sacred and humans are the stewards, guardians and witnesses with a mandate to protect life is fundamental for sustainable innovation. Loss of species diversity is an indicator of the state of human stewardship (*amanah* and *istikhlaf*).

- *Nature is a book of signs*: The evidence of creation in the environment is referred to as '*ayat*' (signs). This is the same word used to describe the verses of the Quran. This urges the human mind to reflect on the signs of creative nature as being expressions of the Divine creativity, and thus as being holy in their very substance.

- *Everything in nature praises God:* The dynamic forms of life bring a new consciousness (*taqwa*) of the meaning, value and purpose of life.

- *Transforming the human consciousness is a pre-requisite for development and prosperity.*

Human-induced activities result in climate change, waste and pollution. The digital world is sinking into a state of nature deficit disorder, which is evident in the model of development and consumerism. In the name of development, humans change the landscape and ecosystems through overconsumption and the production of waste. The consequences of human actions are reflected in severe floods, droughts, species extinction, habitat destruction, climate change and desertification. This notion is clearly explained in the Quran: "Corruption (imbalance) has appeared on earth and at sea because of what the hands of people have wrought; in order that God may make them taste the consequences of their actions; so that they might rethink" (Quran, Surat Al-Rum, 30: 41), and, "Truly God will not change the condition of a people until they change themselves" (Quran, Surat Al-Ra'd, 13: 11).

Naturalistic intelligence can be attained by being mindful of the purpose, value, beauty, order and harmony in the universe and nature. This realization will be reflected in positive action to respect and harness the principles of sustainable innovation.

From all the above principles of environmental stewardship, based on the Quran, we can develop a holistic approach for sustainable innovation which is multi-dimensional and encompasses the cosmos, nature and humans as shown in Table 3.1.

Table 3.1 Principles and implications of eco-innovation and sustainability (Source: Al-Jayyousi, 2016)

Concept/discipline	Implication for eco-innovation
1. Economics of innovation	Evolutionary economics and a shift in the demand curve
2. Environmental policy	Alignment of eco-innovation with public policy to address market failures
3. Product and process innovation	Green businesses inducing radical innovation
4. Sustainability	Green growth and eco-industry creating jobs through SMEs, eco-clusters and eco-parks
5. Open and user innovation	Enhanced abundance and diversity of possible ideas, concepts and eco-solutions
6. Green economy and green growth	Shift in consumption patterns and reduction of ecological footprints to address climate change risks and generate green jobs
7. Knowledge co-creation	Process-based innovation like sustainability reporting, cleaner production, CSR and eco-labelling
8. Corruption and the role of humans	Balance regained through response, learning, adaptation and negative feedback
9. Green business model	Harnessing of the water, energy, food nexus and ecosystem services
10. Human security	Mainstreaming of human and environmental security by valuing ecosystems and natural solutions

3.3 Eco-cosmic innovation and design

The cosmos, ecology, the human body and every living organism together represent a step in the journey for integral innovation. These are open labaoratories and an "open source" of learning and reflection which is critical for a transition to an innovative nation. Viewing the cosmos and ecology as an open source for learning and reflection is essential in a digital era where iPhones and social media tend to limit our live interaction with the web of life. The key concern of a global education is to enable society to respect, appreciate and learn from both the cosmos and ecology. In essence, I see the story of the creation of the cosmos and humans as being about imagination and eco-innovation, regardless of one's views on evolution, creation or intelligent design. The key question is how education systems can be aligned to absorb the lessons embedded in the cosmos and ecology.

> There is instruction for you in cattle. From the contents of their bellies, from between the dung and blood. We give you pure milk to drink, easy for drinkers to swallow.
>
> (Quran, 16: 66)

Reading the above verse is illuminating since it highlights a process and a product to consider as a locally-made business model. This approach is similar to biomimicry, which is a new field of study for R&D and eco-innovation. Designs inspired from nature represent models for sustainable technological innovations since they are responsive, efficient, resilient and eco-friendly. Janine M. Benyus (2002) highlighted a number of examples of eco-innovations in the publication titled *Biomimicry: Innovation Inspired by Nature*:

- Birds cross the globe with a minimum amount of fuel (3 grams);

- A bat uses an efficient transmitter that competes with modern human-made radar technology;

- Birds have been using navigation systems since long before humans invented the GPS.

In sum, we see from this that the journey of innovation is simply a path for achieving excellence (*ihsan*) which is in essence a pursuit of beauty and innovation. As we have discussed before, the use of technology has resulted in spillover effects and externalities; hence, eco-innovation is important in shaping an agenda for inquiry into technology management and innovation. The argument for green innovation and green growth is that environmental considerations and constraints are likely to induce eco-innovations and green technologies as indicated in the case studies below.

3.4 The theory of eco-innovation

The perception of nature and the environment has changed through time due to the scientific revolution and enlightenment. Some early perceptions viewed nature as a "machine" working according to mechanical laws and having infinite resources that could be expanded through technology. This in turn resulted in a model of development that exploited natural resources and caused pollution and waste.

In the 1970s, there was a new awareness and realization that there are limits to growth and it is imperative to rethink our mental model and worldview towards nature. This shift in mindset led to new ways of thinking about the relationship between humans and nature and the role of STI to encompass the notion of *not only learning about nature, but rather also learning from nature*. Consequently, several concepts emerged that called for mainstreaming the environment in decision making and policy domains considering the value of ecosystem services, environmental economics, natural capitalism, biomimicry, the sustainability index, the green economy and the circular economy. Reforming the business models and development thinking to be informed and reformed by nature was a response to the new knowledge in basic and applied sciences, in space sciences and in ICT and to the immense level of environmental degradation. Innovation inspired by nature was driven by the sustainability principles and conditions for progress without having negative impacts on the natural capital.

Cleff and Rennings (1998) articulated a theory for eco-innovation that is informed by neoclassical and evolutionary notions. They argued for the need to enhance knowledge about innovation processes for sustainability by utilizing environmental and economic policy. To assess efficiency, new classical theory can offer insights to frame a sound eco-innovation policy within a social and institutional context. Hence, it is imperative to align eco-innovation policy with environmental policy and strategies to achieve sustainability and prosperity. It is important to understand and mainstream the concepts of innovation for a number of reasons:

- The demand for conservation and lower environmental footprints requires change in both environmental technology and policies.

- Innovation is expected to offset the externalities that result from environmental laws and legislations.

- Sustainability is a multi-dimensional target which requires a holistic approach beyond technology; it requires macro-shifts in consumption patterns and eco-efficiency.

Eco-innovations can be at the product, process, position or paradigm level. However, providing a climate and culture of innovation requires organizational innovation. Eco-innovations involve all sections of a society in developing new ideas, products and processes which make a transition to sustainability. This includes cleaner production and clean technologies. However, incremental and systemic innovations are likely to be framed by business models and organizational settings as articulated by Machiba (2010) and shown in Figure 3.2.

Technology push and market pull are relevant to the domain of eco-innovations as argued by (Pavitt 1984). In principle, the green technology is driven by technology push factors, while consumer preferences for green products are considered as part of market pull factors. However, a well-articulated environmental policy is needed to balance both factors of technology push and market pull. Norgaard and Dixon (1986) have derived some general rules from a co-evolutionary perspective for designing projects which may be applicable to a policy of eco-innovation. These include:

- Ensure diversity.

- Experiment with pilot projects or prototypes.

- Adopt adaptive and flexible approaches.

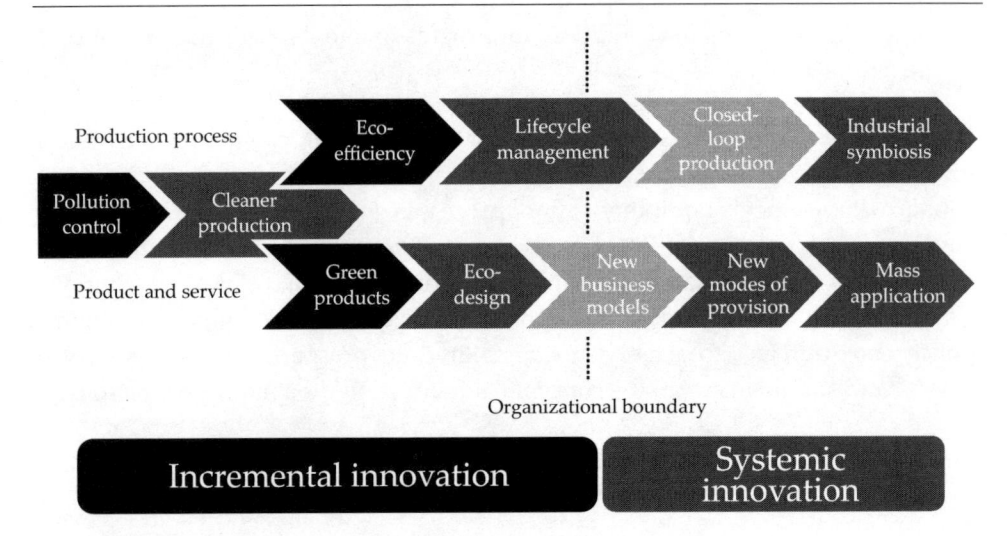

**Figure 3.2   Incremental and systemic innovation processes
(Source: OECD, 2010)**

Kemp (1997, p. 310) suggests adopting a strategy to define a niche which is intended to protect new emerging technologies as in the case of subsides for wind energy technologies in Denmark.

In sum, there are close linkages and seamless connections between ecology, culture and innovation. Eco-innovation was a driving force in shaping the Islamic worldview which is linked to value-based organizations and societies. The challenge remains to what extent humans are able to reflect, learn and mimic nature in a society that is digital and virtual. Humans need to exploit this open source of innovation, nature, to ensure a sustainable human civilization.

3.5 Eco-innovation for sustainability

Natural capital underpins human existence and prosperity. The history of the early civilizations of Africa and Asia during the sixth and eighth century was defined and united by eco-trade along the Silk Road as described by Christian (2000). However, market globalization, population growth and consumerism are exerting immense pressures on the natural capital which is manifested in pollution, waste production, desertification and climate change. In essence, the cycles of economic collapses, poverty, and climate change are clear indicators of market failure. This motivated the emergence of a paradigm shift which includes ideas like the green economy and the circular economy to respond to market failures. The green economy is inspired by concepts of eco-innovations which are founded on the following ideas:

- Invest less;

- Innovate more;

- Generate a stream of cash flows;

- Nurture social capital;

- Support entrepreneurship.

The Green Economy initiative is supported by evidence and business cases in many parts of the globe (Barbier, 2012). The rationale of this initiative is inspired by several success stories that are underpinned by ecological solutions to achieve food, energy and human security in global firms like IKEA, Siemens, Unilever, GE, Toshiba, Google and SEKEM. The green economy unlocks the human potential and imagination to embody eco-innovation at many fronts including product, process, organizational, market, open, user and paradigm innovation. There is evidence that major cities aspire to make a transition to a low-carbon economy and are willing to make investments in green technology to support green transport, green buildings, clean energy, green supply chain, energy efficiency and waste management.

Globally, a number of knowledge products were documented to showcase the value added by eco-innovations (Hamdouch and Depret, 2010). Some illustrative examples include the following:

- Ecological restoration and forest management in India and Nepal;

- Solar energy in Tunisia which was supported by public and investment policy;

- Organic agriculture in Uganda and North Africa;

- A feed-in tariff in Kenya which generated revenue and supported rural development;

- Small-scale renewable energy projects which created new jobs and SMEs in China;

- The conversion of carbon dioxide into nutrition using a photo-bioreactor to produce algae in Austria;

- Bamboo and wetlands utilized to clean up wastewater;

- The use of recycled plastic in construction and buildings;

- The manufacture of eco-friendly leather tanned with titanium rather than chrome.

Nature is the infrastructure and bedrock for economic and human development. For example, medicinal plants provide possible solution for anti-cancer as an alternative medicine (Amin and Mousa, 2007). Human security-mangrove linkages were documented in the case of the tsunami in Asia (Walters, 2008). Greening agriculture contributes positively to climate change mitigation and food security as documented by Hall and Dorai (2010).

Moreover, Sarkar (2013) argues for the need for the adoption of eco-innovation so as to promote sustainable development through harnessing and taking on initiatives and new business models in eco-technology, eco-industry, eco-efficiency and green growth. Eco-innovations may encompass product, process, and open and user innovation. Green activities inspired from eco-innovations are intended to improve green competitiveness by developing green technology, reuse of recycled wastewater and the development of eco-products and food packaging. The benefits of eco-innovations include reducing environmental costs through using less material and energy which in turn reduces ecological footprints and carbon dioxide emissions.

It is insightful to have a fresh look at nature as an open laboratory for eco-innovation. Ecology provides the basics for human wellbeing and livelihoods including water, energy, food, medicine and shelter. The ecological concepts like diversity, optimal allocation and efficiency are validated through the value-added nature of ecosystem services and, hence, can offer new business models for business. In addition, the business case for eco-innovation is clearly manifested in developing eco-industrial parks and clusters of eco-innovation. Specifically, the following are some examples of eco-innovations based on the United Nations Environment Programme (UNEP) Green Economy and Green Growth initiatives (Barbier, 2010).

- Global trade in organic farming amounted to about 54 billion dollars in 1999;

- Siemens uses of clean-technology, wind turbines, resulted in reducing by 4 million tons the carbon dioxide emissions per year;

- Germany has plans to expand development of wind energy to amount to 10,000 Giga-watts by 2020;

- The SEKEM group in Egypt developed commercial compost by considering the lifecycle in supply chain management, which contributed to green jobs and climate change mitigation;

- Unilever's sustainability plan aims to decouple growth from energy use to improve social benefits, reduce ecological footprints and enhance eco-efficiency;

- Green financing for SMEs was adopted by Equity Bank in Kenya and green bonds were developed in the Islamic banking system in Malaysia and the United Arab Emirates (UAE).

Moreover, the transition to a low-carbon economy hinges on eco-innovations in key sectors including infrastructure, agriculture, energy, education, R&D, industry, community and policy arenas. The green economy global initiative is intended to mainstream eco-innovation in all sectors and has a mandate to achieve the following:

- Develop green business models for eco-innovation in all sectors;

- Induce policy reform in both industry and environment;

- Access capital for clean tech and eco-industries;

- Influence the business community to embrace a culture of sustainable innovations;

- Provide business cases for eco-innovation as a sound investment opportunity;

- Raise profit margin and resource efficiency;

- Mainstream eco-innovations in production and consumption;

- Provide evidence of the linkages between human and environmental security;

- Promote science-policy discourse for eco-innovation for sustainable development.

Pauli (2014) highlighted several examples in ecosystem services and eco-innovations in water, energy, food and human security. These examples include:

- Natural vaccines extracted from species;

- Organic pesticides;

- Algae for waste treatment;

- Ecological solutions to descaling water pipes;

- Natural silk for industrial uses.

An integrated seawater, agriculture and energy system in the UAE and Qatar sheds light on the water-energy-food nexus through an application of eco-innovation, as documented by Böer and Adeel (2017). The project uses coastal seawater to raise fish and shrimp then utilizes the nutrient-rich wastewater of the aquaculture to fertilize the oil-rich halophyte plants. This plant in turn is used to produce biofuel for the aviation industry as shown in Figure 3.3.

Eco-innovation inspires ideas and applications in many sectors including industry, business, technology and construction. The work of Egyptian architect, Hasan Fathy, is a good example of harnessing ecology and culture for building housing for the poor. His model of construction in the village of Gourna was unique since it used local mud to build bricks to promote people-centred development and to provide decent housing for the poor (Fathy, 2010). The key characteristics of Hasan Fathy's green construction model include the following:

- Duality of the role of architect as a builder and a craftsman;

- Confluence of tradition and modernity;

- Unity of change and stability;

- Consideration of climate and construction;

- Linkage between society and architecture;

- Introduction of a socio-economic development model.

In addition, eco-innovations play a critical role in developing a green business model that defines value propositions and meets users' demand. These innovations may take the form of a number of process-oriented initiatives. These include:

- Corporate social responsibility;

- Green reporting;

- ISO-green standards.

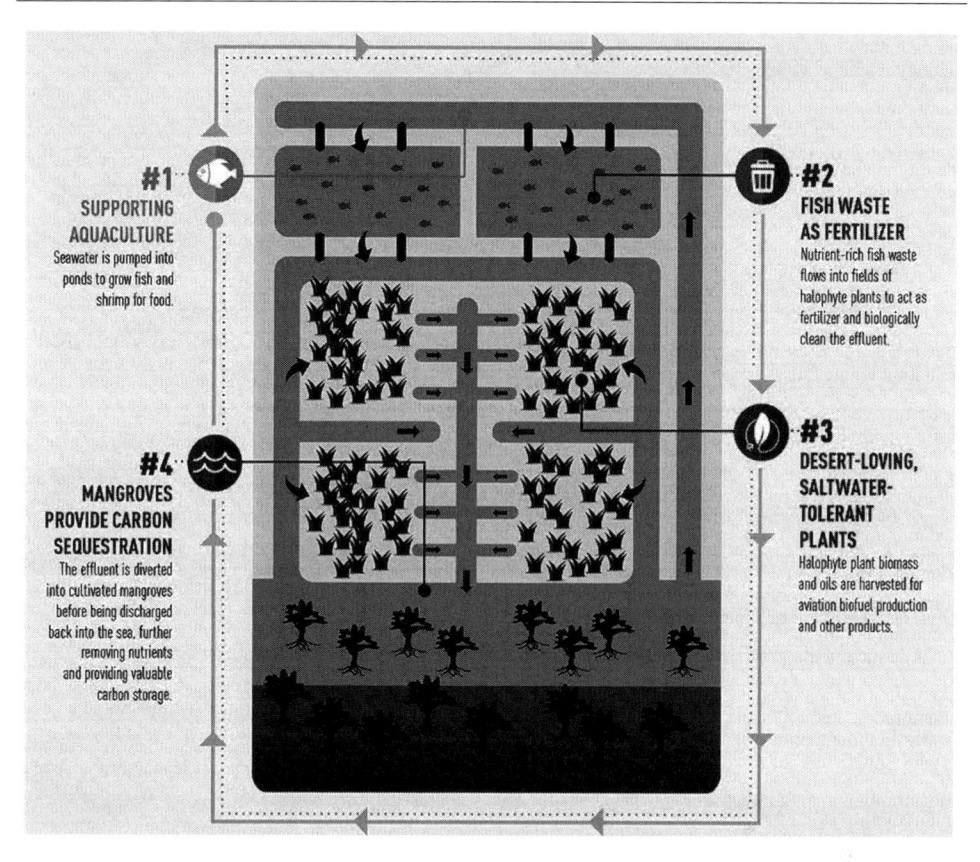

Figure 3.3   Schematic presentation of the integrated seawater energy and agriculture system, UAE and Qatar (Source: http://www. greenaironline.com/news.php?viewStory=2033)

What is enlightening is that fact that the greener the business model, the higher the likelihood of a radical innovation. Models from industry and the public sector illustrate the value of eco-innovation that is inspired from nature and culture to promote sustainable development and citizenship. The model of IKEA represents a good example of a global business that is inspired by nature and respects the sustainability principles. The model is a holistic approach that views eco-design as a competitive advantage. IKEA uses recycled carbon dioxide to save water and it developed a waterless textile dyeing system. The IKEA eco-model embraces the following eco-principles:

- Use of recycled products;

- Adoption of waste management;

- Use of the life-cycle approach;

- Provision of sustainable and affordable solutions;

- Harnessing of open and user innovation;

- Emphasis on diversity and change.

In sum, eco-innovation can inform new models for transforming the economy, society and business environment. The paradigm of eco-innovation is likely to frame a new discourse for sustainability, infrastructure development, environmental policy, innovation theory, social responsibility, knowledge creation and human security. The following is a synthesis of the key relationships or linkages between eco-innovation and sustainable development:

1. The economics of eco-innovation is justified in the light of market failures as seen in climate change and poverty. In addition, a new economic model is to be co-created since the increase of the economies of scale is not likely to reduce the marginal cost.

2. The success of the model of eco-innovation is dependent on crafting an adequate environmental policy. A sound policy should be based on decoupling growth from energy use and environmental externalities. City eco-innovations and the transition to a low-carbon and smart city are underpinned by smart public and environmental policy.

3. Mainstreaming eco-innovations in a strategic and purposeful manner is likely to induce radical innovation.

4. Eco-innovations for achieving sustainable development enable an ecosystem for change in business model, operations and governance. Green SMEs play a crucial role in job creation, sustainability and green growth.

5. Eco-innovation is enriched and complemented by open and user innovation since ecological solutions are inspired by abundance and diversity of ideas and concepts.

6. Harnessing models of eco-innovations contributes to addressing the global challenge of climate change and reducing ecological footprints.

7. The process of eco-innovation provides immense opportunities for knowledge creation and knowledge integration which are of value to eco-industries and green businesses in terms of green certification, trade, eco-labelling and standards.

8. New business models for innovation are likely to emerge from applying eco-innovation in business, the public sector and the community.

9. Eco-innovation presents a business case for economic and social resilience and sustainability. It also provides a model for corporate and social responsibility.

10. Human security and environmental conservation are interlinked and inseparable. Eco-innovation supports new perspectives on people-centred development and the value of natural and social capital in the provision of ecosystem services and human security. The role of mangroves in Asia in reducing and mitigating risks of tsunami is an example of the connection between humans and nature.

References and related bibliography

Al-Faruqi, I. (1998). *Islam and Other Faiths*. A. Siddiqui (ed.); Leicester: The Islamic Foundation, and Herndon, VA: International Institute of Islamic Thought.

Ali, W. (1996). *What is Islamic Art?* Mafraq: Al- al Bayt University.

Al-Jayyousi, O. R. (2016). *Islam and Sustainable Development: New Worldviews*. Abingdon: Routledge.

Amin, A. and Mousa, M. (2007). Merits of anti-cancer plants from the Arabian Gulf region. *Cancer Therapy*, 5, 55–66.

Azzam, K. (2006). *The Principles and Philosophy of Islamic Art*. Available online at: www.mullasadra.org [Accessed 30 September 2014].

Ball, P. (2001). Life's lessons in design, *Nature* 409, 413–416.

Barbier, E. B. (2010). *A Global Green New Deal: Rethinking the Economic Recovery*. Cambridge: Cambridge University Press.

Barbier, E. B. (2012). The green economy post Rio+ 20. *Science*, 338(6109), 887–888.

Benyus, J. (2002). *Biomimicry: Innovation Inspired by Nature*. New York: William Morrow and Company, Inc.

Bess, P. (2003). *The City and the Good Life. The Christian Century*. The Christian Century Foundation. Available online at: www.christiancentury.org [Accessed 15 July 2014].

Blazejczak, J., Edler, D., Hemmeiskamp, J. and Jaenicke, M. (1998). Environmental Policy and Innovation: An International Comparison of Policy Patterns and Innovation Impacts. In: *FlU – Forschungsverbund innovative Wirkungen umweitpolitischer Instrumente (Joint Project on Innovation Impacts of Environmental*

Policy Instruments). *Innovation Impacts of Environmental Policy Instruments.* Synthesis report of a project commissioned by the German Ministry of Research and Technology (BMBF), Volume W. Berlin: Analytica-Verlag.

Böer, B. and Adeel, Z. (2017). Summarizing the Story. In: *The Water, Energy, and Food Security Nexus in the Arab Region.* Switzerland: Springer International Publishing, pp. 223–229.

Capra, F. (1997). *The Web of Life: A Scientific Understanding of Living Systems.* Port Moody, BC: Anchor.

Capra, F. (2002). *The Hidden Connection. A Science for Sustainable Living.* New York: Doubleday.

Cary, J. (1998). Institutional innovation in natural resource management in Australia: The triumph of creativity over adversity. In: *Abstracts of the Conference, Knowledge Generation and transfer: Implications for Agriculture in the 21St Century.* Berkeley, CA: University of California-Berkeley, June 18–19, pp. 11–13.

Christensen, J. F. (1995). Asset profiles for technological innovation. *Research Policy,* 24(5), 727–745.

Christian, D. (2000). Silk roads or steppe roads? The silk roads in world history. *Journal of World History,* 11(1), 1–26.

Cleff, T. and Rennings, K. (1998). Determinants of eco-innovation behavior at the firm level and the role of environmental policy instruments – New empirical evidence from the Mannheim Innovation Panel and an additional telephone survey. Paper prepared for the 7th International Conference of the Greening of Industry Network in Rome, Italy, November 15–18, 1998.

Davies, P. (1984). *Superforce: The Search for a Grand Unified Theory of Nature.* New York: Simon and Schuster Inc.

Denton, M. (1998). *Nature's Destiny: How the Laws of Biology Reveal Purpose in the Universe,* New York: The Free Press, pp. 12–13.

Dosi, G. (1988). The nature of the innovation process. In: Dosi, G., Freeman, C., Nelson, R., Silverberg, O. and Soete, L. *Technical Change and Economic Theory.* London: Pinter Publishers, pp. 221–238.

Fathy, H. (2010). *Architecture for the Poor: An Experiment in Rural Egypt.* Chicago, IL: University of Chicago Press.

Foltz, R. (2013). Ecology in Islam. In: *Encyclopaedia of Sciences and Religions.* Dordrect: Springer Netherlands, (p. 661).

Freeman, C. (1992). *The Economics of Hope.* London and New York: Pinter Publishers.

Fussier, C. and James, P. (1996). *Driving Eco Innovation: A Break through Discipline for Innovation and Sustainability.* London: Pitman Publishing.

Green, K., McMeekin, A. and Irwin, A. (1994). Technological trajectories and R&D for Environmental Innovation in UK Firms. *Futures,* 26, 1047–1059.

Guessoum, N. (2012). Issues and agendas of Islam and science. *Zygon®,* 47(2), 367–387.

Hall, A. and Dorai, K. (2010). *The Greening of Agriculture: Agricultural Innovation and Sustainable Growth.* Available online at https://www.oecd.org/tad/sustainable-agriculture/48268377.pdf [Accessed 15 December 2016].

Hamdouch, A. and Depret, M. H. (2010). Policy integration strategy and the development of the 'green economy': foundations and implementation patterns. *Journal of Environmental Planning and Management*, 53(4), 473–490.

Hawking, S. (1988). *A Brief History of Time*, London: Bantam Press, pp. 121–125.

Hemmeiskamp, J. (1997). Environmental policy instruments and their effects on innovation. *European Planning Studies*. 2, 177–194.

Hemmeiskamp, J. (1998). Innovation Impacts of Environmental and Technology Policy on Wind Energy. In: *Flu - Forschungsverbund innovative Wirkungen umweltpolitischer Instrumente (Joint Project on Innovation Impacts of Environmental Policy Instruments). Innovation Impacts of Environmental Policy Instruments.* Synthesis Report of a project commissioned by the German Ministry of Research and Technology (BMBF), Volume N. Berlin: Analytica-Verlag.

Hölldobler, B. and Wilson, E. O. (1990). *The Ants*. Cambridge, MA: Harvard University Press.

Husaini, W. (1999). *The Quran for Astronomy and Earth Exploration from Space*, 3rd ed. New Delhi: Goodword Press.

Jaffe, A. B. and Palmer, K. (1996). *Environmental Regulation and Innovation: A Panel Data Study*. Washington, DC: National Bureau of Economic Research. Working Paper 5545.

Kemp, R. (1997). *Environmental Policy and Technical Change*. Cheltenham and Brookfield, VT: Edward Elgar.

Kiuchi, T. and Shireman, B. (2001). *What We Learned in the Rainforest: Business lessons from nature*. Oakland, CA: Berrett-Koehler Publishers.

La'li, M. (2004). *A Comprehensive Exploration of the Scientific Miracles in Holy Quran*, Victoria, BC: Trafford Publishing, pp. 35–38.

Lovins, A. B., Lovins, L. H. and Hawken, P. (1999). *A Road Map for Natural Capitalism*. Available online at https://msuweb.montclair.edu/~lebelp/ALovinsNatural CapitalismHBR1999.pdf [Accessed 15 July 2015].

Machiba, T. (2010). Eco-innovation for enabling resource efficiency and green growth: development of an analytical framework and preliminary analysis of industry and policy practices. *International Economics and Economic Policy*, 7(2–3), 357–370.

Moore, K. (1982). *Developing Human: Clinically oriented embryology*, 3rd ed. Philadelphia, PA: W. B. Saunders Company.

Moore, K. L., Johnson, E. M., Persaud, T. V. N., Goeringer, G. C., Zindani, A. M. A. and Ahmed, M. A. (1992). *Human Development as Described in the Qur'an and Sunnah*, Makkah: Commission on Scientific Signs of the Qur'an and Sunnah.

Nasr, S. H. (1996). *The Meaning and Concept of Philosophy in Islam*. Available online at http://www.muslimphilosophy.com/ip/nasr-ip1.htm [Accessed 15 May 2015].

OECD. (1992). *OECD Proposed Guidelines for Collecting and Interpreting Technological Innovation Data - Oslo-Manual*, OECD/GD(92)26. Paris: OECD Publishing

OECD. (2010). *OECD Science, Technology and Industry Outlook 2010*. Paris: OECD Publishing.

Pauli, G. (2014). *The Blue Economy: 10 Years, 100 Innovations, 100 Million Jobs*. Taos, NM: Paradigm Publications.

Pavitt, K. (1984). Sectoral patterns of technical change: towards a taxonomy and a theory. *Research Policy*, 13, 343–373.

Rennings, K., Koschel, H., Brockmann, K. L. and Kuehn, I. (1999). A Regulatory Framework for a Policy of Sustainability – Lessons from the Neoliberal School. *Ecological Economics*. 28(2), 197–212.

Sagan, C. (1983). *Cosmos*, Avenel, NJ: Wings Books, pp. 5–7.

Sarkar, A. N. (2013). Promotion of eco-innovation to leverage sustainable development of eco-industry and green growth. *International Journal of Ecology & Development™*, 25(2), 71–104.

Stoneman, P. (1983). *The Economic Analysis of Technological Change*, Oxford: Oxford University Press.

Tirole, J. (1989). *The Theory of Industrial Organization*, Cambridge, MA: The MIT Press.

Walsh, V. (1996). Design, innovation and the boundaries of the firm. *Research Policy*, 25(4), 509–529.

Walters, B. (2008). Mangrove forests and human security. *CAB Reviews*, 3(64), 1–9.

Wescoat, J. L. (1995). From the Gardens of the Qur'an to the Gardens of Lahore. *Landscape Research*. 20, 19–29.

Yahya, H. (2004). *The Qur'an Leads the Way to Science*, 2nd edition. Istanbul: Global Publishing, pp. 69–72.

Zaidi, I. H. (1981). On the Ethics of Man's Interaction with the Environment, *Environmental Ethics*, 3(1), 35–47.

Zayd, N. A. (2006). *Reformation of Islamic thought: A critical historical analysis* (Vol. 10). Amsterdam: Amsterdam University Press.

4

Technical innovation

Appropriate technology is an outcome of social construction which leads to locally-rooted tools, methods and culture of innovation.

(The author)

4.1 Introduction

This chapter builds on the previous chapters which addressed cultural and ecological innovations. Progress is a result of transferring ideas to products and profit through technological innovations, the manifestation of these innovations will be operationalized through technical/technological and economic innovations. This in turn will lead to sustainable innovation through individual, communal, organizational and national innovations as indicated in Figure 4.1.

Historically, after the Enlightenment in Europe, science and technology were perceived as a panacea for resolving all human suffering from poverty to health and livelihood. The notion of a "technological fix" was challenged in the last five decades by Kuhn in his work, *The Structure of Scientific Revolutions* (Kuhn and Hawkins, 1963), in which he argues that theories have meaning within a dominant paradigm.

However, technologies evolve with societies (Saviotti, 2005) and people improve and adapt appropriate tools and methods to make their lives efficient and easy. Moreover, the externalities which result from the applications of some technologies like nuclear energy and the environmental costs due to degradation of ecosystems led to a process of rethinking the rationale and contribution of technology to sustainable development. The linear model of technological innovation (referred to as technological determinism), which is based on the concept that "science invents, technology applies and market selects", was replaced by theories like that of the social construction of technology, where technological innovation is shaped by the meaning that a society develops based on context and problem definition.

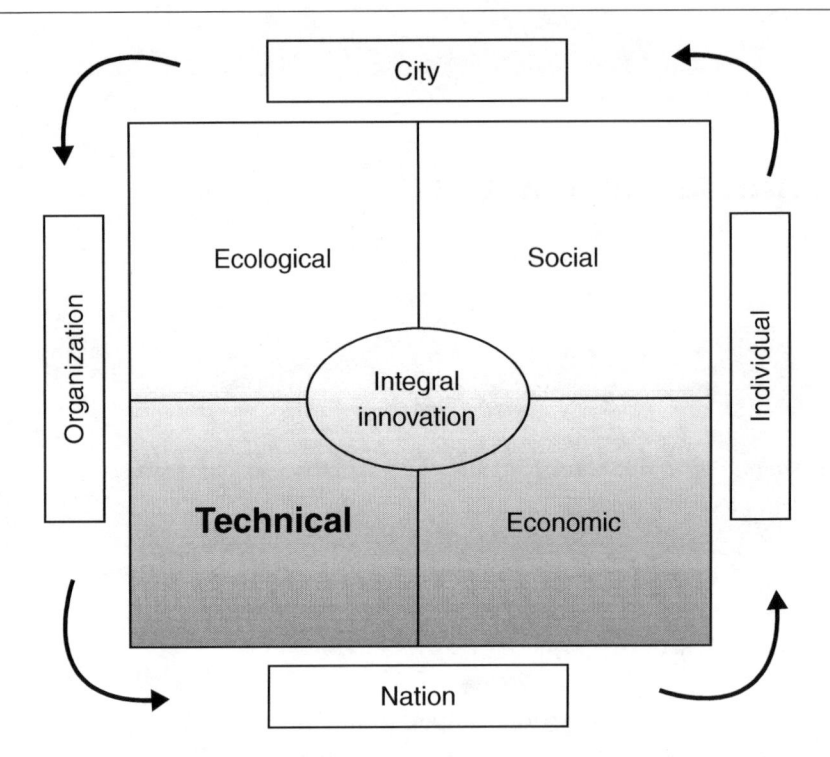

Figure 4.1   A model for integral innovation focusing on technical innovation

Technological developments influence society and vice versa. Lee and Mathews (2013) argue that STI play a critical role in speeding up the process to make a shift to sustainability. They pointed out that latecomer countries can harness the positive outcomes of STI if they adopt appropriate strategies and policies such as leapfrogging, where they can integrate up-to-date technology and jump to a new paradigm. To do so, countries need to develop an enabling environment of STI systems and intellectual property rights that supports and promotes technology transfer and diffusion.

The notion of a technological fix and the belief that "market forces determine the development of science and technology" have been contested since they overlook the role of society and national policy in technology development. However, in order that technological innovation contributes to sustainability, *it is imperative to align technology policy with the national development agenda.* This will enable developing countries to promote the use of sustainable technologies through the adoption of an innovation policy. The science-policy interface implies that we see the synergy and connection between policy choices for sustainable economic development and technological innovation.

Figure 4.2 illustrates a conceptual framework of the linkages between the three domains of sustainable development (social, economic and ecological) along with

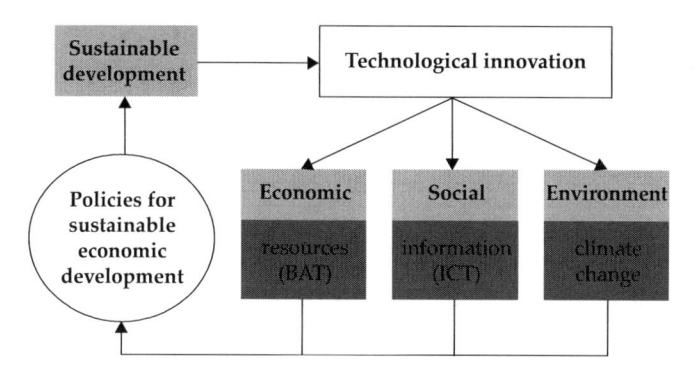

Figure 4.2   A framework for linking sustainable development and technology (Source: Constantinescu and Frone, 2014)

policies, technological innovation and best available technologies (BATs) supported by ICT. A framework like this would contribute to the enhancement of technological innovation for water, environment, food and climate change.

Rahman (1981) studied the interaction of science and technology with society viewed from a historical and socio-political perspective through the European experience in Asia. He pointed out that Francis Bacon outlined how science and technology shape society and development through painting a future outlook for a prosperous society and economy. This vision was justified based on the idea that science and technology are considered as an independent force in society. It was thought that developments in science and technology would lead to the modernization of society. Hence, the transfer of science and technology by Europe to the developing world was driven by a modernization agenda. In addition, science and technology were considered socially, politically and ethically neutral. It was believed that technological developments would lead to human prosperity. However, these hopes have not been fully realized due to the unintended consequences of technology.

It is alarming to realize that science and technology were viewed as European phenomena. It is argued that the contributions of the Islamic civilization during the medieval era were not highlighted and hence technology was used as a means for intellectual hegemony. David Arnold (2005) in his work "Europe, technology, and colonialism in the 20th century", reviewed the history of technology and its linkages to European colonialism. He argued that technologies were developed and diffused by Europe with limited input from local people. The conventional belief was that, if technologies did not offer the intended promise, this was due to the inability of local people to use and appreciate the benefits of technology.

The history of technology may be traced back to the start of European colonialism since this is linked to major transformations in technology, economics and politics.

Specifically, the rice cultivation in Asia was associated with technologies in water and irrigation that enabled and supported colonial powers. In medicine, Chinese medicine, which had a long legacy and unique approach to treatment, was influenced by the Western school of thought and lost its roots.

The transfer of technology from Europe to the developing world was realized during the mid to late nineteenth century and continued through colonialism until World War I, during which time the control of diseases like malaria was enabled by advanced medicine, sanitation and public health. Other major technologies like railroads and telegraphs shaped the notion of a dominant Europe in all domains of life. This led to the notion of technology as a key determinant of history (e.g., Cameron, 1967; McClellan and Dorn, 2015). Machines thus became the universal "measure of men" (Adas, 1990) and historians have now become aware of the deep and implicit ideological uses of imperial technology (Arnold, 1993).

It is argued that technologies like the railways, irrigation systems and the telegraph were symbols of imperial dominance to command respect and control of the local people. These Western technologies replaced the local technologies and had major impacts on culture, economy and ecology. In addition, after the independence of many developing countries following World War II, decolonization and popularization of technologies accelerated the export and diffusion of technologies to the developing world including cars, telephones, television, agricultural and health technologies. This was evident in India, Africa, and the Middle East where, to some people and nations, technology was viewed as alien and linked to colonial power (Goonatiliake, 1984; Nandy, 1988; Shiva, 1991).

In essence, the paradigm of development that emerged after World War II had deepened the technological gap between the West and the developing world. The gap between "local knowledge" and "Western scientific knowledge" was widened due to the horizontal transfer of technology between East and West (Agrawal, 1995; Gupta, 1998). In the case of Oman, the horizontal transfer of technology reached fruition only because when the Sultan of Oman established a sugar mill in Zanzibar the local human capital was developed. In contrast, a dependency model was established in Egypt during the Mohammad Ali era in 1805 where technology was founded on Western expertise and later collapsed when it relied on the capacity of local people. The Japanese model of technology transfer promoted the development of the capacity of technical human capital, which in turn contributed to a culture of technology becoming mainstream in a number of societies in the MENA region.

Economic growth and progress is underpinned by technological innovations and a nation's economy reflects the level of technological innovations. The nature of technology may be viewed as evolutionary and incremental as argued by Arthur

(2009). However, its development and progress is defined by standard operational techniques and assembly of inventions which is similar to Kuhn's notion of normal science. This means that there is no stand-alone technological breakthrough but a combination of many inventions and innovations. New technologies are simply constructed from existing ones.

The speed and pace of technological change due to green technologies and the introduction of ICT and new web-based platforms and business models are accelerating technological obsoleteness. In addition, the global changes as manifested in financial crises, disease, poverty and climate change present a challenge to technological innovations and the limits of what technology can resolve in terms of human prosperity and control of the natural and human environment. In sum, in order to instil a culture of technological innovation, it is imperative to promote people-centred development models where local people embody the ethos of innovation. This is part of a decolonization process that is necessary to overcome the dependency model of development and limit the historical process of technological hegemony. The developing world has an opportunity to mainstream green technology and this entails innovations in all domains of the economy, environment and society.

4.2 Innovation and green technology in the developing world

A transition to green technology and a lower carbon economy was articulated as a global response to climate change risks and environmental pollution and waste. Harnessing green technological innovations was defined as a measure to mitigate environmental risks. SMEs play a crucial role in job creation and economic development. A paradigm shift in the economic development model was articulated including the circular and green economies. The concepts of the green economy and eco-innovations were envisioned to mainstream environmental technologies and green practices in industry and society.

At the global level, funding of climate change adaptation and mitigation is mainly available through the United Nations Convention on Climate Change and the Clean Development Mechanism (CDM) and the Global Environment Facility. In the MENA region, there are some initiatives in green technology utilizing the CDM and the Adaptation Fund. The CDM is a provision of the protocol including incentives and funded projects to speed up a transition to clean production through reducing carbon emissions. Clean production projects are linked to a scheme of carbon credit for a reduction of CO2 (Pereira de Carvalho and Barbieri, 2012). Also, the concept of the energy service company has been implemented in countries such as Egypt and Tunisia, and Lebanon's Central Bank has mechanisms in place to facilitate financing for some limited renewable energy projects. This in turn has opened market opportunities for SMEs to engage in green technologies.

The MENA and GCC regions are characterized by water scarcity, energy dependence and unemployment. These challenges demand a policy reform and a shift to a green economy and changes in production and consumption. This structural change implies a "pull" towards participation in green technology and a "push" towards market needs. The GCC represents the oil-producing countries which include Saudi Arabia, the UAE, Oman, Qatar, Kuwait and Bahrain. However, this region is investing in the knowledge economy and is keen to transform to a low-carbon economy that is underpinned by innovation (ESCWA, 2015).

Despite the fact that the MENA region is one of the key players in two sectors, the oil industry and water desalination, it was not able to establish innovation clusters and an enabling environment, including technology infrastructure, consultancy, SMEs and services related to these sectors. Currently there is a potential to nurture a new business model for green SMEs that addresses the supply chain so as to provide green jobs and promote green innovation in the region.

To harness the comparative advantage of the private sector in green business and sustainable innovation, corporate social responsibility (CSR) programmes and financial tools such as environmental taxation and pricing, green financing and economic incentives are key enablers to facilitate the adoption and diffusion of green technology (Hasper, 2009). In addition, civil society institutions play a crucial role in the transition towards green business through green procurement, business incentives and green financing.

The notion of Green Knowledge Nodes, referred to as Green Help Desks (GHDs) was initiated by the United Nations Economic and Social Commission for West Asia (ESCWA) in 2012 so as to provide a linkage between green suppliers and customers and to support SMEs in entering the market. Five GHDs were established in Egypt, Oman, Tunisia, Jordan and Lebanon. It was evident that many countries in the region lacked a regional platform for green services to advocate and support strategies for green business and knowledge transfer.

It is critical to establish regional innovation hubs (RIHs) in the MENA and GCC regions and to foster and enable open and user innovations so as to strengthen the capacity of national and local governments and support the production sectors, particularly SMEs, to engage in the emerging green economy sectors, including eco-tourism, waste management, renewable energies, forestry, organic farming and cleaner production. Specifically, the RIHs will have the mandate to support local institutions and SMEs to align their strategies and programmes with green economy strategies; facilitate knowledge sharing of green practices; and enhance organizational and technical capacity for national entities to formulate green policies and programmes.

One of the key challenges is to define the necessary conditions for enhancing the sustainability of the RIHs in the MENA and GCC regions to support green technology for SMEs through open and user innovation. A paradigm shift has emerged in innovation management that has transformed the conventional closed and linear model, as shown in Figure 4.3, to open and user innovation as shown in Figure 4.4. This shift was informed by technology and market forces so as to ensure a sustainable business model and comparative advantage. Open innovation was referred to and adopted in many disciplines including business, technology and engineering. This notion was cited extensively in the last decade since it became relevant to the market conditions, strategy and business models.

A holistic view of open and user innovation was developed which entails combining knowledge from external and internal domains in a cyclic model that is underpinned by entrepreneurship, as shown in Figure 4.4. In addition, a number of studies articulated different models of innovation including those by Gabison and Pesole (2014); Baldwin and von Hippel (2009); and Chesbrough (2003). Open innovation was also viewed as a model that entails both user and social innovations. To capture the complexity of innovation clusters, system analysis and social networks were proposed by Cândido (2012) to study the dynamics of open innovation.

Christensen, et al. (2005) assessed and commented on a variety of models in open innovations based on technology, industry and organization, as in the cases of IBM (Chesbrough, 2007) and Procter and Gamble (Huston and Sakkab, 2006). However, the critical question remains when and where to use open innovation to leverage the internal or external knowledge to develop competitive advantage. Sawhney and Nambisan (2007) identify four models of open innovation. These include the "Orchestra" model as illustrated in the global network adopted by Boeing which consists of over 700 partners; the "Creative Bazaar" model which

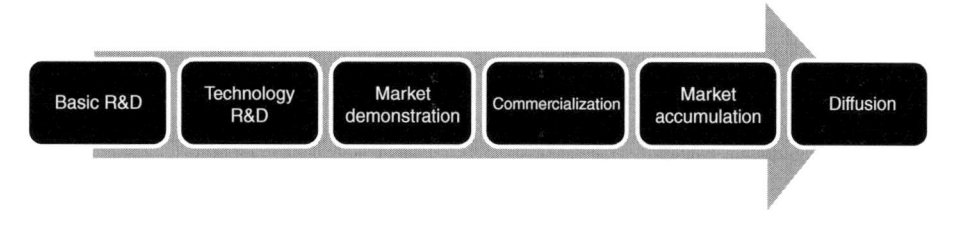

Figure 4.3   A linear model of innovation (Source: Wiesenthal, et al., 2009, citing Grubb, 2004)

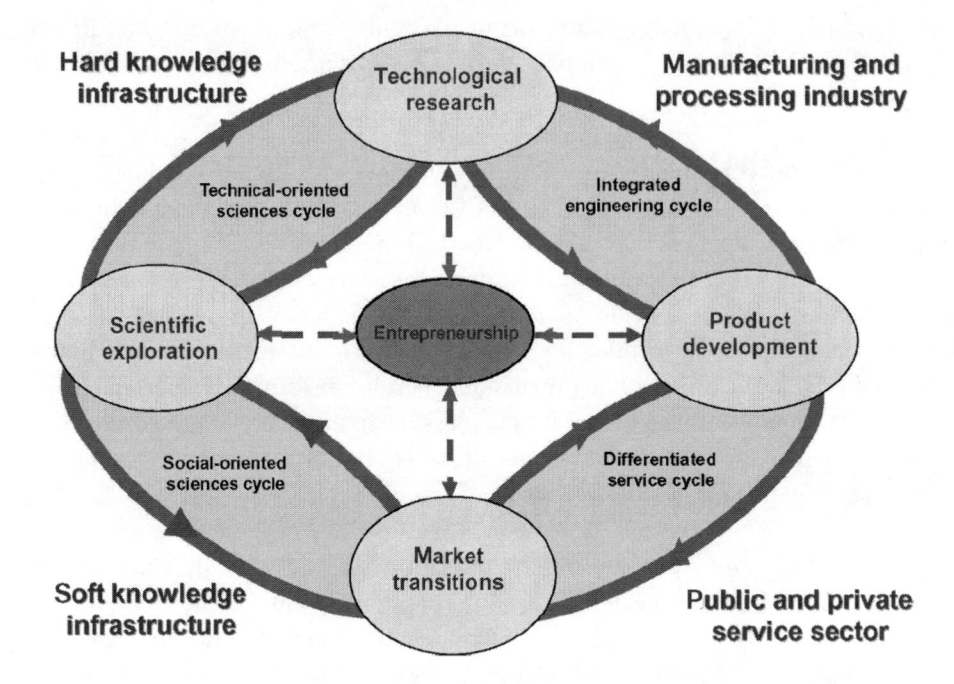

Figure 4.4 Cyclic innovation model based on system thinking and entrepreneurship (Source: Van der Duin, Ortt and Kok, 2007)

involves a form of crowdsourcing as used by P&G in the Innocentive.com approach; the "Jam Central" model which is based on creating a central vision and harnessing inputs from different stakeholders; and the "MOD Station" model which encourages external users to induce innovations as applied in the BBC and Lego (2007). All of these are keen to build a business model that utilizes internal and external knowledge to create value. Yet, the challenge is how to find the right partners and how to work with them.

To address environmental challenges and climate change, green technologies and eco-innovations for SMEs were devised. Breitzaman and Thomas (2011) concluded that SMEs outperformed large firms in patent growth and contribution to economic growth. In addition, Pereira de Carvalho and Barbieri (2012) argued for sustainable innovation and eco-innovation throughout supply chains in industry to achieve economic, social and environmental objectives. Hasper (2009) argued for promoting green technology through global exchange platforms to overcome trade barriers and IP controls in developing countries.

Two case studies follow on green technology and energy security.

4.3 Case study 4.1: Open innovation for green SMEs in the GCC region

The MENA region is faced with multi-faceted challenges related to water, energy, food and climate change. These challenges are compounded by the socio-economic constraints due to urbanization, unemployment and governance deficits. In addition, the indicators for STI and R&D are below global standards, the ecological footprint for the Arab region is high in the oil-rich countries as reflected in the consumption patterns (ESCWA, 2015).

Bahrain is a small country in the GCC but it has rich institutional and human capitals. In addition, Bahrain has sound financial institutions and an infrastructure for SMEs, this includes Bahrain Economic Development Bank, the SME unit within the Ministry of Industry, the Chamber of Commerce and Industry, and the United Nations Industrial Development Organization (UNIDO) Industrial and Technology Promotion Office. Moreover, Bahrain has an enabling environment and infrastructure for business and technological innovation; this includes: the Bahrain Business Incubator Centre which is financed by the Bahrain Development Bank, and the Tamkeen and Bahrain Development Bank. Several banks provide funds for SMEs including Kuwait Finance House, First Investment Bank, Venture Capital Bank, Gulf One Investment Bank and Addax.

In addition, the mission of Arabian Gulf University (AGU) is to be a model for higher education in water, environment, biotechnology, and technology and innovation management. The ambition of the AGU is to become one of the leading academic innovation hubs by providing quality education that inspires innovation. Hence, the AGU is positioned to act as a regional hub for STI and green technologies in the MENA region. This hub can support the mission of the existing GHDs and mainstream green technology and STI in SMEs by providing added-value services in renewable energy, forestry, eco-tourism, organic farming, green ICTs, green buildings and solid waste management. The regional hub for GHDs will support each knowledge node in capacity building and knowledge sharing of best practices in SMEs business models.

The proposed RIH in Bahrain is envisioned to support the achievements of the UN sustainable development goals (SDGs) through activating the existing GHDs in Lebanon, Jordan, Tunisia, Iraq, Egypt and Oman and establishing a new GHD in Bahrain for the promotion of green technologies. The GHDs in the MENA region are currently undertaking several activities related to waste management, eco-tourism, renewable energy, green buildings, green ICTs, e-waste management, green procurements and resource efficiency. There are initiatives in the region to develop green technologies based on the water-energy-food nexus to ensure sustainable development. The untapped potential of renewable energy for job creation should be unlocked since the rate of development of renewable energy is less than 8 per cent, compared to a global average of approximately 19 per cent (AUE, 2012).

SMEs are playing a significant role in job creation (Nicola, 2009), technology transfer and transition to a green economy (Di Tommaso, Lanzoni and Rubini, 2001). In Egypt, SMEs are the backbone of the economy, where they contribute to almost 80 per cent of GDP to the non-agriculture sector and provide 75 per cent of the private sector employment, mostly in manufacturing and retail trades (Di Tommaso, 2001). In Jordan, SMEs represent 98 per cent of all companies registered and contribute about 50 per cent of GDP (Al-Mahrouq, 2010). In Lebanon, SMEs account for 99 per cent of the economic activity and contribute to 82 per cent of the total employment in the country. Hence, the regional hubs can harness STI to unlock the potential of the human, industrial, financial and social capitals to achieve SDGs.

Key partnerships were formed for the GHDs in each country as reflected in the main hosting entities for GHDs, as seen in Table 4.1: the ALI in Lebanon, the RSS in Jordan, the CEDARE in Egypt, the Ministry of Sustainable Development in Tunisia and the Public Authority for SMEs in Oman. These host entities provide the appropriate ecosystem and habitat for networking, outreach, fundraising and policy influence.

The regional hub for STI and green technologies is designed to strengthen and complement on-going efforts in each country to conserve ecosystems and natural

Table 4.1   Partnerships hosting GHDs in the MENA region

Stakeholder agency	Type of partnership
Ministry of Environment and Sustainable Development, Tunisia	The Ministry is the lead government agency for environmental policy development and management. Where it does not have a direct operational role, it still functions in an advisory capacity for GHDs in Tunisia.
Royal Scientific Society (RSS), Jordan	The RSS is entrusted with the oversight of cleaner production centres, R&D and consultations in water, energy and the environment.
Public Authority for SME development, Oman	The Authority has recently been assigned responsibility for SME development and planning in Oman and is therefore a crucial partner for the GHDs.
Association for Lebanese Industrialists (ALI)	ALI is a union for all industries in Lebanon and is linked to policy making processes to support businesses and SMEs to be resilient and competitive.
Centre for Environment and Development for the Arab Region and Europe (CEDARE), Egypt	CEDARE is a hosting GHD in Egypt and has a programme on water, the environment and the private sector. It has sound national, regional and global links to R&D and funding entities.

resources by mainstreaming green technologies and innovation in development sectors including water, energy, construction and agriculture. Through the regional hubs, the GHDs will ensure that the investment made in realizing the national development strategies integrate green businesses and SMEs in development policy.

The regional hubs will seek to support and inform national regulatory frameworks, backed by an effective enforcement system and founded on sound management standards. The marketing for the GHD services is informed by national mandate which makes it easy to communicate key messages to the public and private sectors. The national sustainability plans and GHDs' operational plans address cross-cutting priorities, namely, 1) the need for well-documented information and knowledge bases for green businesses and services; 2) the need for an integrated SMEs green business investment environment; 3) capacity development and technical training; and 4) public awareness initiatives.

The RIH is based on open and user innovation that utilizes both internal and external knowledge. The regional hub can harness the potential of green procurement, CSR, green banking, climate change funds and offset programmes. Moreover, the RIH also can contribute to accessing regional funding through development banks in the region by supporting SMEs in eco-initiatives including pilot renewable energy projects, cleaner production, green construction, e-waste management, energy and water audits, eco-labelling and capacity building. There is evidence that the technical expertise in Lebanon and Jordan was disseminated to Oman through sharing knowledge and services between GHDs. Cross-fertilization and generation of new ideas for green SMEs were experienced through regional fora and workshops. Co-creation of ideas and sharing of tacit knowledge took place among GHDs with the support of UN bodies and the private sector.

In order to facilitate the creation of new market opportunities, the RIH can support the introduction and use of environmentally sound technologies to enhance resource efficiency and reduce waste. The market penetration of appropriate green technologies should be considered a priority in the MENA region hosting the GHDs. The strategic intent of the regional hubs is to provide a platform for knowledge sharing and networking for green business. This implies the need to ensure access to new and emerging markets, reduce production costs across the value chain, attract financial resources and increase productivity and technical capacity. Moreover, the regional hub will serve as a networking platform to match green investors and venture capital with green businesses in the region.

In essence, the RIH is intended to address the imperatives for developing an integrated strategy and funding model which includes strategic alignment of the UN ESCWA Sustainable Development Productivity Division, the UNIDO Bahrain office and GHDs within the six countries. In addition, having proper alliances with R&D institutions, funding entities, the private sector and civil society is crucial for sustaining the GHDs. Overall, the regional hub aims to achieve the following:

- *Strategic level*: Support GHDs with alignment of their actions plans programmes and projects with green economy strategies and related national plans and strategies on green jobs, sustainable consumption and production patterns, sustainable procurement and CSR.

- *Advocacy on STI and green technologies*: Foster a knowledge-based economy to ensure the transition to a green economy. It is critical that each GHD has the capacity to support local communities and governments in evidence-based solutions and best practices.

- *Knowledge management*: Facilitate knowledge sharing of green practices, methods and approaches at both national and regional levels among GHDs.

- *Capacity building*: Enhance organizational capacity and technical skills for GHDs to formulate green policies and programmes and to ensure their implementation. Each GHD should have a core competence to share with others in the network.

POLICY IMPLICATIONS AND NECESSARY CONDITIONS

A compelling and transformative vision that enhances regional innovation networks is the key to instilling a climate of innovation. Moreover, BATs supported by ICTs contribute to enhanced eco-efficiency and enable social change through social media, e-learning and e-government models. Technologies to address climate change like carbon capture and storage are vital for sustainability. However, it is critical that this framework is supported by an ecosystem with sound institutional and human capital. A shift to green business implies the following:

- *Regional knowledge sharing*: The fluctuation of global oil prices has substantial ramifications for trade, business and consumption and production patterns which in turn affect water and ecological footprints. The consequences of the reduction of oil prices by about 60 per cent during 2015 are affecting global supply and demand of energy and food supplies. In addition, the discovery of oil shale in the USA is likely to affect the global energy market in the Middle East since the USA will be among the top three oil producers along with Saudi Arabia and Russia (IRENA, 2015). In essence, regional policies should consider the comparative advantage within countries and be formulated to enhance social cohesion, economic resilience and environmental sustainability. Green SMEs have a business opportunity and can provide a business case for a sustainable economy. A policy for energy diversification and investment in renewable energy is critical for sustainable development in the MENA region (Sowers, et al., 2011). Hence, promoting regional cooperation along the water, energy, food nexus is essential to achieve effective climate change mitigation measures through investment and utilization in renewable energy and valuing ecosystem services in light of the Climate Summit in 2015 (Gleick, 2014).

- *Green and decent jobs*: Utilizing green businesses and technologies for renewable energy for water and construction contributes to meeting the growing energy demand, reducing the negative impacts of climate change and providing job opportunities for SMEs. Certified vocational training is essential to enable young professionals to access the job market.

- *Funding models for SMEs*: There are a number of funding opportunities for green SMEs through green funds, governmental programmes and international agencies. However, there is a need to support SMEs in business planning, proposal development and project management.

- *Technical support for SMEs*: Technological innovations play a critical role in the transition to a sustainable mode of development. The RIH can harness the positive outcomes of green technology and provide capacity building programmes for SMEs which include both business skills and technical know-how. Hence, it is crucial that each national GHD identifies its core competencies in light of the local context, needs and players. The GHD will be demand driven and respond to clients' needs which may include services and goods in the domain of energy and water technologies, construction and waste management.

In sum, the sustainability plan for the RIH entails ensuring the provision of an enabling environment, political commitment, a funding model and strategic partnerships. Moreover, to ensure sustainability, it is critical to ensure proposer linkage to cleaner production centres (CPCs) and partnerships with universities and R&D entities. The hosting institutions should reap the benefits and values of having a GHD and this in turn will be reflected in their commitment to sustaining operations. Personal interviews and field visits to the GHDs in the five countries revealed that, to ensure sustainability, a set of conditions must be met. These include linking with CPCs at both the national and regional level through joint activities; developing the capacity in proposal development and building partnerships with regional funding entities (e.g., IDB, Arab Fund, Kuwait Fund) and multi-lateral or UN coalitions; branding, packaging and marketing green services and products to key partners and stakeholders; and developing a system for audits, learning, and monitoring and evaluation.

The RIH has a mandate to optimize resource use and mainstream green SMEs that are less polluting, more resource efficient, have reduced emissions and are able to compete in local and export markets in the development sectors. The domains of sustainability include the following:

- *Environmental sustainability*: The GHD will address environmental protection and the planned interventions will ensure that green business for SMEs is in line with the principles of sustainability. Hence, SME development will not exist in biodiversity sensitive areas, and that impacts are reduced, mitigated and offset as necessary elsewhere, thus reducing pressures on biodiversity. The RIH will also transform the investment practices of private sector investors to SMEs. This will change the development trajectory of the green business sector – ensuring the compatibility of production practices with green economic strategy. The sustainability of biodiversity's contribution (ecosystem services) to the viability of the green industry will be assured through the mutual gains and benefits that are to be made.

- *Institutional sustainability*: The RIH will influence the policies and investments of several government agencies responsible for green business and SME development. The regional innovation model will support a culture of green business through leverage and scaling up of best practices. At the same time, capacity will be enhanced to secure the implementation and application of the new tools. Since the new developments will be carried out with the full participation of local government, R&D and civil society, a deep sense of ownership will be generated.

- *Financial sustainability*: The RIH will be making the case for all stakeholders to start seeing green SMEs as making economic as well as ecological sense. Recognition of the economic value of biodiversity together with the ownership that will be achieved in the green products/services will lead to a protective stance from the industry, and this will augur well for the sustainability of the project products, services and benefits.

- *Regional linkages*: The regional network of green innovations in the MENA region is critical to support processes of knowledge management, leverage funding, learning and marketing services and technical expertise across the Arab countries. This will help develop alliances with R&D and CPCs and support the initiation of clusters of excellence where expertise can be harnessed across the region. Moreover, the regional linkages will help access and leverage funds from regional banks or through UN networks.

ACKNOWLEDGEMENT

This research was based on technical support and funding support from the UN ESCWA Sustainable Development Productivity Division, Lebanon, 2014.

4.4 CASE STUDY 4.2: ENERGY AND TECHNOLOGICAL INNOVATION IN THE ARAB REGION

What is the trade-off between renewable energy and nuclear energy in the Arab region? How can innovations in green technology shape a new discourse for the MENA and GCC region? Energy security is one of the defining issues for sustainable development and progress for any region. Open innovation in energy technology is likely to influence trade and development policy in light of the demand from China and India and the emergence of new energy sources like oil shale in the USA and natural gas.

The GCC region is rich in oil and gas since it has about 56.8 per cent of proven reserves of crude oil and 26.51 per cent of proven natural gas reserves worldwide. However, diversifying the energy mix to include solar and nuclear energy is imperative. Some countries have a high appetite for risk in terms of adopting nuclear energy as in the case of the USA, France and Japan where their economies use 22 per cent, 85 per cent and 65 per cent of nuclear energy, respectively (Tae-gyu, 2011). On the other hand, India and China rely heavily on coal for electricity production. They are investing in nuclear energy to achieve energy security (Delfeld, 2010). In the MENA and GCC region, Saudi Arabia, Jordan, Egypt and the UAE are planning to include nuclear energy as part of their energy mix (Laurent, 2008). The crucial question is what the key innovations in energy technology and energy efficiency will entail in terms of public policy in the GCC and MENA region in the twenty-first century to address both energy security and climate change risks. Can renewable energy induce a form of disruptive technology?

Energy consumption in the GCC is one of the highest worldwide. Demand for oil in the GCC region grew fivefold in the last four decades (World Bank, 2013). Investing in renewable energy has a positive effect on the economy and job creation. The shift to renewable energy is likely to be constrained by a number of factors; these include fluctuations in oil prices in the global market, the environmental cost due to the use of fossil energy, and energy subsidies in the GCC region. Innovation policy is underpinned by public policy and economic incentives. The energy subsidies to fossil energy create market distortion and limit possibilities for making renewable energy economically feasible. In 2012, the solar energy price in the GCC ranged from 11–48 cents per kilowatt/hour for large installations using photovoltaic cells. Since the tariffs for industrial and commercial uses are 35 cents per kilowatt hour and 133 cents per kilowatt hour, respectively, this makes the use of renewable energy feasible in the industrial and commercial sectors (Al-Jayyousi, 2015).

The GCC region is investing in infrastructure for science and technology but it is still below the global scale in terms of number of patents. The centre of gravity in science and technology is shifting towards the GCC. This is evident in the scale of investment in infrastructure for science and technology in the Kuwait Institute for Scientific Research (KISR), the Qatar Foundation, Masdar City and the King Abdullah University of Science and Technology. This in turn is likely to provide an ecosystem to foster opportunities and constitute a critical mass and a tipping point to catch up and leapfrog technology. To make a transition to renewable energy requires transforming innovative ideas into products and profits.

References and related bibliography

Adas, M. (1990). *Machines as the Measure of Men: Science, Technology, and Ideologies of Western Dominance*. Ithaca, NY: Cornell University Press.

AFED. (2011). *Arab Environment 4; Green Economy: Sustainable Transition in a Changing Arab World*. Beirut. Available online at http://www.afedonline.org [Accessed 19 July 2012].

African Development Bank (ADB). (2011). *Gender, Poverty and Environmental Indicators on African Countries*. Volume XII, Tunis: Economic and Social Statistics Division, ADB.

Agrawal, A. (1995) Dismantling the divide between indigenous and scientific knowledge. *Development and Change*, 26, 413–439.

Akeel, R. (2013). *Supporting Innovation in SMEs in Lebanon through a Public/Private Equity Fund: The ISME Fund*. Available online at http://pubdocs.worldbank.org/en/242771479323031491/QN81.pdf [Accessed 10 September 2014].

ALI (Association of Lebanese Industrialists). (2012). *The Industrialist's Journey Companion*. Newsletter 1. Association of Lebanese Industrialists. Available online athttp://www.ali.org.lb/uploads/projects/pdf/ALInews2012-2.pdf [Accessed 30 April 2013].

Al-Jayyousi. O. R. (2001). Capacity building for desalination in Jordan: necessary conditions for sustainable water management. *Desalination*, 141, 169–179.

Al-Jayyousi, O. R. (2015). *Renewable Energy in the Arab World: Transfer of Knowledge and Prospects for Arab Cooperation*, Amman: FES.http://library.fes.de/pdf-files/bueros/amman/11667.pdf.[Accessed 10 August 2016].

Al-Mahrouq, M. (2010). *Success Factors of Small and Medium-Sized Enterprises (SMES): The Case of Jordan.* Available online at http://www.acarindex.com/dosyalar/makale/acarindex-1423869515.pdf [Accessed 15 October 2014].

Al-Saleh, A. (2012). *Exploring Strategies for Small and Medium Enterprises in Saudi Arabia*, RIBM Doctoral Symposium on "Strategies for SMEs in Saudi Arabia", 14–15 March 2012. Available online at http://www.greengrowthknowledge.org/sites/default/files/downloads/resource/ESCWA_MAPPING%20GREEN%20ECONOMY%20IN%20THE%20ESCWA%20REGION.pdf [Accessed 12 August 2014].

Arab Research Forum (ARF). (2009). *Arab Knowledge Report 2009*, ARF. Available online at https://www.google.com.bh/webhp?sourceid=chrome-instant&ion=1&espv=2&ie=UTF-8#q=ARF.+(2009).+Arab+Knowledge+Report+2009%2C+Arab+Research+Forum+(ARF) [Accessed 11 June 2014].

Arnold, D. (1993). *Colonizing the Body: State Medicine and Epidemic Disease in Nineteenth-Century India.* Berkeley, CA: University of California Press.

Arnold, D. (1996). *The Problem of Nature: Environment, Culture and European Expansion.* Cambridge, MA: Blackwell Publishers.

Arnold, D. (2005). Europe, technology, and colonialism in the 20th century. *History and Technology*, 21(1), 85–106.

Arthur, W. B. (2009). *The Nature of Technology: What it is and how it evolves.* New York: Simon and Schuster.

AUE (Arab Union of Electricity). (2012). *Statistical Bulletin 2011*, 20th issue. AUE.

Baldwin, C. and von Hippel, E. (2011). Modeling a paradigm shift: From producer innovation to user and open collaborative innovation. *Organization Science*, 22(6), 1399–1417.

Cameron, R. (1967) Imperialism and Technology. In: Kranzberg, M. and Pursell, C. W. (eds). *Technology in Western Civilization. Vol. 2, Technology in the Twentieth Century.* New York: Oxford University Press.

Cândido, A. C. (2012). Open innovation and social network analysis. *Enterprise and Work Innovation Studies*, 8, 41–55.

Chesbrough, H. (2003). The logic of open innovation: managing intellectual property. *California Management Review*, 45(3), 33–58.

Chesbrough, H. W. (2007). Why companies should have open business models. *MIT Sloan Management Review*, 48(2), 22.

Christensen, J. F., Olesen, M. H. and Kjær, J. S. (2005). The industrial dynamics of Open Innovation – Evidence from the transformation of consumer electronics. *Research policy*, 34(10), 1533–1549.

Cohen, W. M. and Levinthal, D. A. (1990). Absorptive capacity: A new perspective on learning and innovation. *Administrative science quarterly*, 35, 128–152.

De Jong, J. P. and von Hippel, E. (2009). Transfers of user process innovations to process equipment producers: A study of Dutch high-tech firms. *Research Policy*, 38(7), 1181–1191.

Delfeld, C. (2010). Global Gambits, *Forbes* (8 February 2010). Available online at http://www.forbes.com/global/2007/0423/024.html [Accessed 15 July 2013].

Di Tommaso, M. R. (2001). *Industry, Policies and SMEs. An Inquiry on some Arab Mediterranean Countries.* Available online at http://www.unido.org/fileadmin/user_media/MEDEX/med_publications_documents/Support_to_SMEs_in_Arab_Region._The_case_of_Tunisia.pdf [Accessed 15 October 2014].

Di Tommaso, M. R., Lanzoni, E. and Rubini, L. (2001). *Support to SMEs in the Arab Region: The Case of Tunisia. UNIDO/UNDP, UNIDO Italy.* Available online at http://www.unido.org/fileadmin/user_media/MEDEX/med_publications_documents/Support_to_SMEs_in_Arab_Region._The_case_of_Tunisia.pdf [Accessed 15 October 2014].

ECORYS. (2012). Ex-post evaluation of Macro Financial Assistance operations to Lebanon. Rotterdam: European Commission, Directorate General Economic and Financial Affairs Available online at http://ec.europa.eu/economy_finance/evaluation/pdf/evaluation_lebanon_en.pdf [Accessed on 1 August 2012].

ESCWA. (2010). *Green Economy Implications of the Sustainable Livelihood Approach for Sustainable Development in the Arab Region,* Expert Group Meeting on Promoting Best Practices on Sustainable rural Livelihoods in the ESCWA Region, 24–25 November, Beirut, Lebanon: United Nations Economic and Social Commission for Western Asia (ESCWA). Available online at css.escwa.org.lb/sdpd/1350/17.pdf [Accessed 30 April 2013].

ESCWA. (2011a). *Sustainable Livelihoods and the Green Economy,* Beirut: United Nations Economic and Social Commission for Western Asia (ESCWA).

ESCWA. (2011b). *Environmental Goods and Services in the ESCWA Region: Opportunities for Small- and Medium-Sized Enterprises,* Beirut, Lebanon: United Nations Economic and Social Commission for Western Asia (ESCWA).

ESCWA. (2014). *Mapping Green Economy in ESCWA Region,* Beirut: United Nations Economic and Social Commission for Western Asia (ESCWA).

ESCWA. (2015). *Role of Technology in Sustainable Development in the Arab Region.* Technical Paper, April 2015. Beirut: United Nations. Available online at http://css.escwa.org.lb/SDPD/3572/5-Technology.pdf [Accessed 20 August 2015].

European Environment Agency (EEA). (2012). *Green Economy,* EEA. Available online at http://www.eea.europa.eu/themes/economy/intro [Accessed 30 April 2013].

Flamos, A., Papadopoulou, A. and Karakosta, C. (2007). *CDM in MENA countries: Strengths, Weaknesses & Opportunities,* 4th Middle East and North Africa Renewable Energy Conference (MENAREC 4), 21–24 June 2007, Damascus, Syrian Arab Republic.

Frone, S. and Constantinescu, A. (2014). Impact of technological innovation on the pillars of sustainable development. *Calitatea,* 15(S1), 69.

Gabison, G. and Pesole, A. (2014). *An Overview of Models of Distributed Innovation. Open Innovation, User Innovation, and Social Innovation* (No. JRC93533). Seville: Institute for Prospective and Technological Studies, Joint Research Centre.

Gassmann, O., Enkel, E. and Chesbrough, H. (2010). The future of open innovation. *R&D Management,* 40(3), 213–221.

Ghadban, R. and Laidler-Kylander, N. (2011). *Souk El Tayyeb: Defying the Line between Business and Non-Profit.* The Fletcher School, Tufts University. Available online at http://www.soukeltayeb.com/souk-el-tayeb-defying-the-line-between-business-and-non-profit/ [Accessed 8 August 2012].

Gleick, P. H. (ed.) (2014). *The World's Water Volume 8: The Biennial Report on Freshwater Resources* (Vol. 8). Washington, DC: Island Press.

Goonatiliake, S. (1984). *Aborted Discovery: Science and Creativity in the Third World.* London: Zed Books.

Grubb, M. (2004). Technology innovation and climate change policy: an overview of issues and options. *Keio Economic Studies*, 41(2), 103–132.

Gupta, A. (1998). Postcolonial Developments: Agriculture in the Making of Modern India. Durham, NC: Duke University Press.

Hala, A. A. and Albin, T. (2012). *The Environment and the Economy in the Arab World.* ERF Policy Research Report no 37. The Economic Research Forum (ERF).

Hasper, M. (2009). Green technology in developing countries: creating accessibility through a global exchange forum. *Duke Law and Technology Review*, 7, 1–14.

Huston, L. and Sakkab, N. (2006). Connect and develop. *Harvard Business Review*, 84(3), 58–66.

IBRD. (2010). *Achieving Sustainable Development in Jordan: Country Environmental Analysis*, Amman: The International Bank for Reconstruction and Development (IBRD)/The World Bank, September 2010.

ILO (International Labour Organization) and UNDP (United Nations Development Programme). (2011). *Green Jobs Assessment in Lebanon: Synthesis Report.* Geneva: International Labour Office. Available online at http://www.ilo.org/wcmsp5/groups/public/---ed_emp/---emp_ent/documents/publication/wcms_168091.pdf [Accessed 18 August 2012].

Jaffe, M. and Al-Jayyousi, O. R. (2002). Planning models for sustainable water resource development. *Environmental Planning and Management*, 45 (3), 309–322.

Kuhn, T. S. and Hawkins, D. (1963). The structure of scientific revolutions. *American Journal of Physics*, 31(7), 554–555.

Laurent, L. (2008). Emirates eager for nuclear, *Forbes* (23 June 2008) Available online at http://www.forbes.com/2008/08/08/homek-abu-dhabi-face-markets-cx_ll_0806 autofacescan01.html [Accessed 1 August 2013].

Lee, K. and Mathews, J. (2015). Toward new rules for science and technology policy for sustainable development 1. Global Governance and Rules for the Post-2015 Era: Addressing Emerging Issues in the Global Environment, 107.

McClellan III, J. E. and Dorn, H. (2015) *Science and Technology in World History: An Introduction.* Baltimore, MD: JHU Press.

Mansour, A. (2011). *Small and Micro Enterprises Development in Yemen and Future Prospects*, Social Fund for Development (SFD). Available online at http://www.sfd-yemen.org/uploads/issues/SMED%20Book%202011-20120716-142650.pdf [Accessed 12 August 2015].

MCI. (2011). *Annual Industrial Report 2011*, Ministry of Commerce and Industry (MCI), Sultanate of Oman. Available online at https://stat.unido.org/admin/publicationPdf [Accessed 12 August 2015].

Merhebi, M. (2011). Legal and Technical Frameworks for Environmental Compliance in Lebanon. In: EFL (Environmental Fund for Lebanon), *Training on Environmental*

Compliance. Beirut, 17 June 2011. Available online at http://www.therefordesign. net/EFL/ [Accessed 3 September 2012].

MOE (Ministry of Environment). (2012). National Report to the United Nations Conference on Sustainable Development (Rio+20). *Sustainable Development in Lebanon: Status and Vision.* Republic of Lebanon. Also available online at http://www.uncsd2012.org/content/documents/758Lebanon%20RIO+20%20Report%20 English.pdf [Accessed 30 September 2014].

MOI (Ministry of Industry). (2010). *The Lebanese Industrial Sector: Facts and Findings 2007.* Available online at http://www.industry.gov.lb/Documents/ Publications%20and%20studies/Study%202007.pdf [Accessed 13 August 2014].

Nandy, A. (ed.) (1988) *Science, Hegemony and Violence. A Requiem for Modernity.* Delhi: Oxford University Press.

Nicola, M. (2009). *Middle East – The rising importance of SMEs,* Special Report GR_20Jul09, Dubai: Standard Chartered Bank. Available online at http://www. dubaibusinessadvisors.com/uploaded_documents/Middle_East_-_The_rising_ importance_of_SMEs_24_08_09_05_38.pdf [Accessed August 2015].

Pereira de Carvalho, A. and Barbieri, J. C. (2012). Innovation and sustainability in the supply chain of a cosmetics company: a case study. *Journal of Technology Management & Innovation, 7*(2), 144–156.

RAC/CP. (2011). *State of the Art of Green Entrepreneurship in Tunisia,* Barcelona, Spain: Regional Activity Centre for Cleaner Production (RAC/CP).

Rahman, A. (1981). The Interaction between Science, Technology and Society: Historical and Comparative Perspectives. *International Social Science Journal, 33*(3), 508–521.

Sakman, S., Wackernagel, M., Galli, A. and Moore, D. (2011). *Sustainable Development and Environmental Challenges in the MENA Region: Accounting for the Environment in the 21st Century.* Economic Research Forum (ERF), June.

Saviotti, P. P. (2005). On the co-evolution of technologies and institutions. In *Towards Environmental Innovation Systems.* Berlin: Springer, pp. 9–31.

Sawhney, M. and Nambisan, S. (2007). *The Global Brain: Your roadmap for innovating faster and smarter in a networked world.* Englewood Cliffs, NJ: Pearson Prentice Hall.

Shiva, V. (1991) *The Violence of the Green Revolution.* London: Zed Books.

Sowers, J., Vengosh, A. and Weinthal, E. (2011). Climate change, water resources, and the politics of adaptation in the Middle East and North Africa. *Climatic Change, 104*(3–4), 599–627.

Stevenson, L. (2010). *Private Sector and Enterprise Development: Fostering Growth in the Middle East and North Africa,* Cheltenham: Edward Elgar International Development Research Centre (IDRC).

Tae-gyu, K. (2011) KEPCO puts safety first in building UAE nuclear plant, *Korea Times.* Available online at http://www.koreatimes.co.kr/www/news/biz/2011/03/ 123_84184.html [Accessed 10 August 2013].

Teece, D. J. (1986). Profiting from technological innovation: Implications for integration, collaboration, licensing and public policy. *Research policy, 15*(6), 285–305.

UNDESA. (2012). *A guidebook to the Green Economy*; Issue 1: Green Economy, Green Growth, and Low-Carbon Development – history, Definitions, and a Guide to Recent Publications. United Nations Division for Sustainable Development (UNDESA). Available online at http://sustainabledevelopment.un.org/index.php?page=view&type=400&nr=634&menu=35 [Accessed 15 September 2014].

United Nations Environment Programme (UNEP). (2012). *Green Economy in a Blue World*: UNEP. Available online at http://www.unep.org/pdf/green_economy_blue.pdf [Accessed 23 September 2015].

UNIDO. (2011). *UNIDO Green Industry Initiative for Sustainable Industrial Development*, Vienna: United Nations Industrial Development Organization (UNIDO), October 2011.

Van der Duin, P., Ortt, R. and Kok, M. (2007). The Cyclic Innovation Model: A New Challenge for a Regional Approach to Innovation Systems? *European Planning Studies*, 15(2), 195–215.

Van de Vrande, V., De Jong, J. P., Vanhaverbeke, W. and De Rochemont, M. (2009). Open innovation in SMEs: Trends, motives and management challenges. *Technovation*, 29(6), 423–437.

Von Hippel, E. (2009). Democratizing innovation: the evolving phenomenon of user innovation. *International Journal of Innovation Science*, 1(1), 29–40.

West, J. and Bogers, M. (2014). Leveraging external sources of innovation: a review of research on open innovation. *Journal of Product Innovation Management*, 31(4), 814–831.

Wiesenthal, T., Leduc, G., Köhler, J., Schade, W. and Schade, B. (2010). *Research of the EU Automotive Industry into Low-Carbon Vehicles and the Role of Public Intervention*. Seville: JRC Technical Notes.

World Bank. (2011). *Republic of Lebanon Country Environmental Analysis*. Available online at http://test.moe.gov.lb/Documents/WB%20-%20Final%20CEA.pdf [Accessed 15 August 2012].

World Bank (2013). *World Development Indicators*. World Bank database. Available online at http://data.worldbank.org/data-catalog/world-development-indicators [Accessed 16 January 2017].

Zahlan, A. B. (1978). *Technology Transfer and Changes in Arab World*, Oxford: Pergamon Press.

5

Economic and business innovation

Economic and business innovation is underpinned by an articulated business model to capture value; product and process innovation are defined and shaped by business models.

(The author)

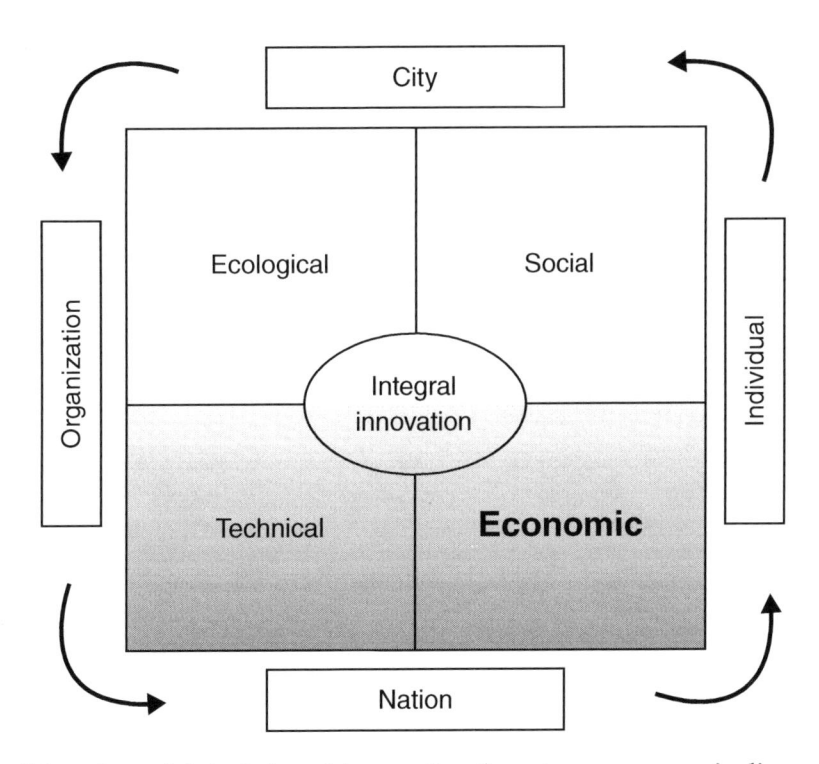

Figure 5.1   A model for integral innovation focusing on economic dimension

5.1 Introduction

This chapter highlights the other dimension of innovation which is linked to economic and business model innovation (see Figure 5.1). The focus will be on business models as a key for innovation management. The notion of "innovation for development" emerged to address the stagnation in the economic business cycle. This makes innovation an appealing field of inquiry and exploration in many disciplines including engineering, economics, business and marketing.

Human progress and prosperity is fuelled by innovations in all spheres of life. Innovations in material science, printing, transport, agriculture, energy and telecommunications have transformed our economy, society and environment. Research into the role and impact of innovation on economic development was initiated in the 1960s in the Science Policy Research Unit at the University of Sussex. There was a realization that innovation requires a cross-disciplinary inquiry to gain insights into the climate and nature of innovation. Specifically, innovation involves not only organizational learning, sociology and management science, but also technology management.

Joseph Schumpeter (1883–1950) was a pioneering thinker in innovation who wrote *The Theory of Economic Development* (1911) and *History of Economic Analysis* (1954) and addressed the role of innovation in economic and social change. He argued that economic development should be viewed as a process that is driven by innovation as manifested in new products, processes, supplies and markets. He stressed the role of entrepreneurship and innovation at both individual and organizational levels. Also, he highlighted the tendency for innovations to "cluster" in certain industries and time periods and the possible contribution of such "clustering" to the formation of business cycles and "long waves" in the world economy (Schumpeter, 1939).

In addition, the intellectual contribution to the theory of innovation can be traced back to the work of Freeman in his books in the 1970s and 1980s, e.g., *The Economics of Industrial Innovation, Unemployment and Technical Innovation* and *Technical Change and Economic Theory*. It was discovered that organized R&D offered a structured focus and was strategic in terms of the direction of technological innovation if based on a national development agenda. However, there are a variety of types of innovation which include user and open innovation, social innovation and service innovation. Also, we should be mindful of the innovations that emerge through action and coincidence. Pavitt (1984) identified different categories of technologies which included high-tech, science-based and specialized suppliers. Each type of technology requires a unique set of enablers, policies and incentives to foster innovations.

The book *An Evolutionary Theory of Economic Change* (1982) by Richard Nelson and Sidney Winter articulated the nature and drivers of innovation. They argued that capitalism is a key motive for innovation. Moreover, they introduced the notion of "bounded rationality" as an ingredient for socio-technological and organizational transformation. Their conceptual models suggested that organizations are informed and guided by routines and procedures. These routines are developed through practice and action across the organization which may hinder or constrain innovation.

5.2 Business model development

A business model describes how an organization defines, articulates, develops and harnesses value (Osterwalder and Pigneur, 2010). The business model proposed by Osterwalder and Pigneur (2010) consists of nine building blocks which include a set of components as indicated in Figure 5.2:

- Users or stakeholders;

- Organizational offerings;

- Systems and institutional infrastructure;

- Financial and funding model.

The nine building blocks that constitute the business model, as illustrated in Figure 5.3, are as follows:

1. *Customer segments* which identify various target stakeholders by using a set of management tools like customer profiles and empathy maps to assess customer demand.

2. *Value propositions* which define the possible benefits and services that a customer may gain through a specific business. For example, eco-innovation can provide a number of benefits and services as outlined in Table 5.1.

3. *Channels* which define the specific ways a firm communicates with various customers and may include communication, distribution and sales channels.

Table 5.1   Business model types and potential impacts on sustainable innovation (Source: Boons, et al., 2013)

Business model types	Potential impacts (second-order effects)		
	Economic	Social/cultural	Environmental
Eco-innovative products	Greener markets and economies	Change in people's preferences towards greener products	Reduced footprint due to use of greener products
Waste regeneration systems	Valorizing waste and new market niche	New jobs, diffusion of knowledge and technology	Linked to prevention of waste, avoided extraction of natural resources
Renewable energy-based systems	Linked to new economic activities	Local employment	GHG emission reduction
Efficiency optimization by ICT	Expansion of ICT sector, new business opportunities		Linked to resource use optimization and saving
Functional sales	New service markets niche	Increased awareness of customers	Reduced footprint due to resource saving and use of greener products/services
Innovating financing	New service markets niche	Increased awareness of customers	Reduced footprint due to resource saving
Sustainable mobility systems	New service markets niche	Flexibility, change in people's preferences and attitudes	Linked to resource use optimization and saving
Industrial symbiosis	Valorizing waste and improved efficiencies		Linked to resource use optimization, symbiotic activities, waste reduction
Eco-cities	Greener markets, new market niches, services. Valorizing waste and improving efficiencies	High-quality life, change in people's preferences and attitudes, new jobs	Linked to resource use optimization, symbiotic activities, waste reduction

4.   *Customer relationships* which describe the forms and types of relationships a firm establishes with specific customer segments. This may range from personal communication to virtual interaction.

5.   *Revenue streams* which represent the financial model that a firm adopts to generate cash from various customers. Revenue may be generated from asset sales, usage fees, subscription fees, leases, licensing, brokerage fees, advertising and auctions.

6.   *Key resources* which include assets needed to enable a business model to function. Assets may be financial, human, intellectual or physical.

7.   *Key activities* which describe the priority actions or tasks a firm should conduct to make the business model functional. Activities may include production, marketing, distribution, R&D and platform management.

8.   *Key partnerships* which describe the network of suppliers and partners that make the business model work. This may be in the form of a partnership, alliance or joint venture.

9.   *Cost structures* which describe the key cost components required to operate a business model.

A number of innovative business models include new web-based platforms like that of iPod/iTunes which is used to provide access to music for the iPod. This platform for the iPod and the online store exemplify disruptive technology. Other business models include the Uber taxi service, Mobile car care, Skype and Nextbike (www. nextbike.de/en). These organizations are characterized by flexibility and system solutions. The key to developing a sustainable business model is understanding customer needs and profiles and aligning them with a value proposition as indicated in Figures 5.2 and 5.3.

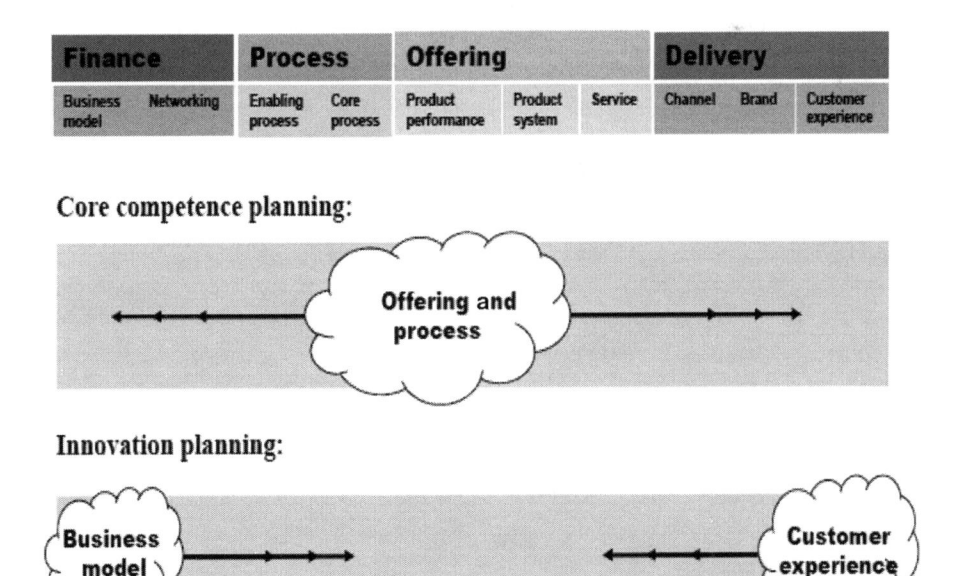

Figure 5.2   Components of a business model for innovation management (Source: Osterwalder and Pigneur, 2010)

Key partners	Key activities	Value propositions	Customer relationships	Customer segments
(access to key resources and activities; reduced de-risking and uncertainty, benefits from economies of scale or improved quality)	(production, services, networking/ brokerage)	(new or improved products and services, cutomization, brand, price, cost reduction, convenience, risk reduction)	(including post-sale services, technical assistance, co-creation)	(mass market, niche market, diversified customer base, etc)
	Key resources		Customer channels	
	(physical including materials and energy, human, financial)		(direct or indirect sales)	

Cost structure	Revenue streams
(cost-driven versus value-driven models)	(asset sales, usage fee, lending, renting, leasing, licensing, brokerage fees, advertising)

Figure 5.3   The key components for business model development (Source: Osterwalder and Pigneur, 2010)

Innovations can be developed in many domains as articulated by Keely, et al., 2013 and depicted in Figure 5.4.

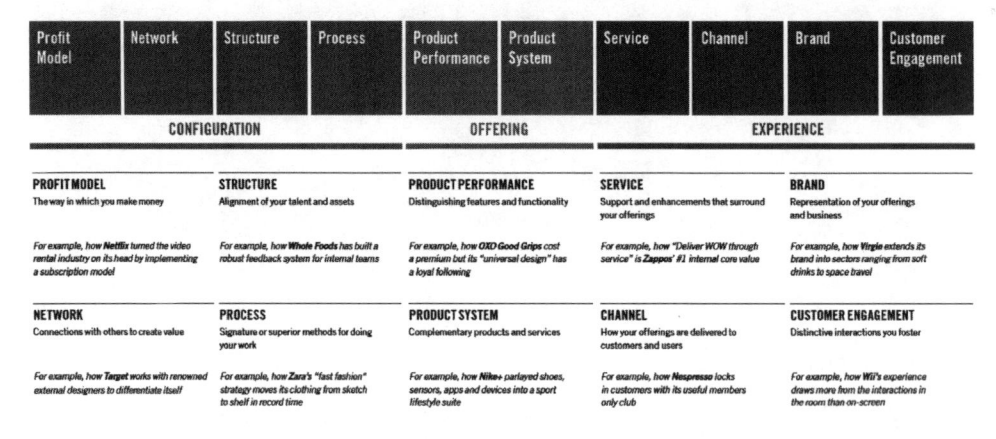

Figure 5.4   A framework for ten types of innovation (Source: Keeley, et al., 2013)

To conclude, the methodology for developing a new business model may be summarized as follows:

1. Assess the existing *business model* by using a structured framework that links the value proposition of the organization with the customer's demands and the financial model. This framework is referred to as the Business Model Canvas.

2. Understand *customers* by using empathy maps and by matching customer profiles with the organizational value proposition which is referred to as a "value map".

3. Develop and assess *new ideas* for a product or process through the following means:

    a. Creativity tools like brain storming techniques;

    b. Learning from competitors;

    c. Systematic problem solving.

4. Create a *new business model*.

Many business models are considered innovative due to their use of web-based platforms for e-banking, e-commerce, e-trade and e-learning. AliBaba is a good example of an innovative global e-commerce model as will be discussed below.

5.3 Models of business innovation

One of the early attempts to conceptualize innovation was carried out by Stephen Kline and Nathan Rosenberg (1986) by developing and commenting on the linear model of innovation. The linear model is based on the assumption that innovation consists of a set of phases that includes *research*, *development*, and *production and marketing*. However, Kline and Rosenberg pointed out the following limitations of the linear model:

1. The linear model generalizes a chain of cause and effect but is limited in its applicability in the domain of innovations;

2. Innovations may result from users, society or even by coincidence or by a combination of a set of inventions;

3. The linear model is likely to overlook some learning from feedback.

The information age has revolutionized business models and the way we conduct business. ICT and web technology has enabled the development of many platforms to support new business models like eBay, Amazon.com, iTunes, Uber, e-government, e-trade, e-banking, Airbnb and e-services. These innovative models have transformed the roles of suppliers and customers. One of the innovative e-commerce models is that of AliBaba. The following is a summary of the AliBaba e-commerce model in China which is used for different types of sales and retail, based on the model of Amazon.com and eBay.

The AliBaba business model of e-commerce follows the motto: "Attract shrimps and the whales will come".

A summary of the key characteristics and strategies of the AliBaba business model, as illustrated in Figures 5.5 and 5.6, is outlined below:

1. Help sellers meet buyers through web-based platforms and tools;

2. Utilize web-based technologies and tools as new platforms where suppliers and manufacturers meet buyers (outsourcers and wholesalers) on a global scale;

3. Consider customers as both sellers and buyers who can post "storefronts" to advertise;

4. Use two languages: Chinese and English;

5. Capture a high market share through competitive costs and diversification;

6. Adopt a flexible and adaptive corporate strategy;

7. Harness the potential of global markets and diversified demand.

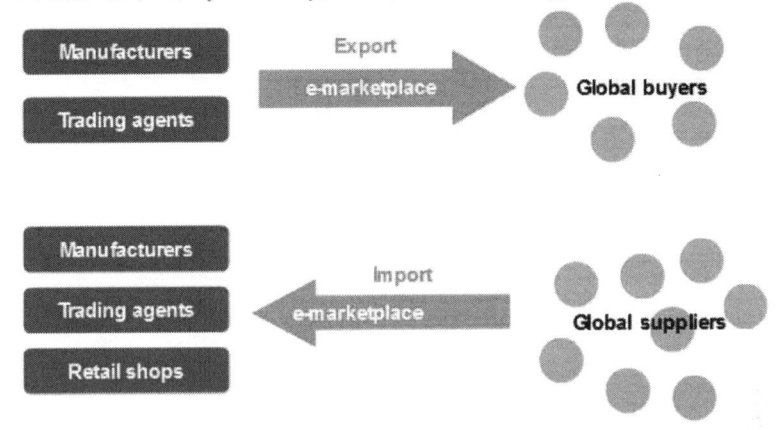

Figure 5.5   AliBaba's business model of open innovation (Source: http://www. jteall.com/Alibaba%2001.pdf)

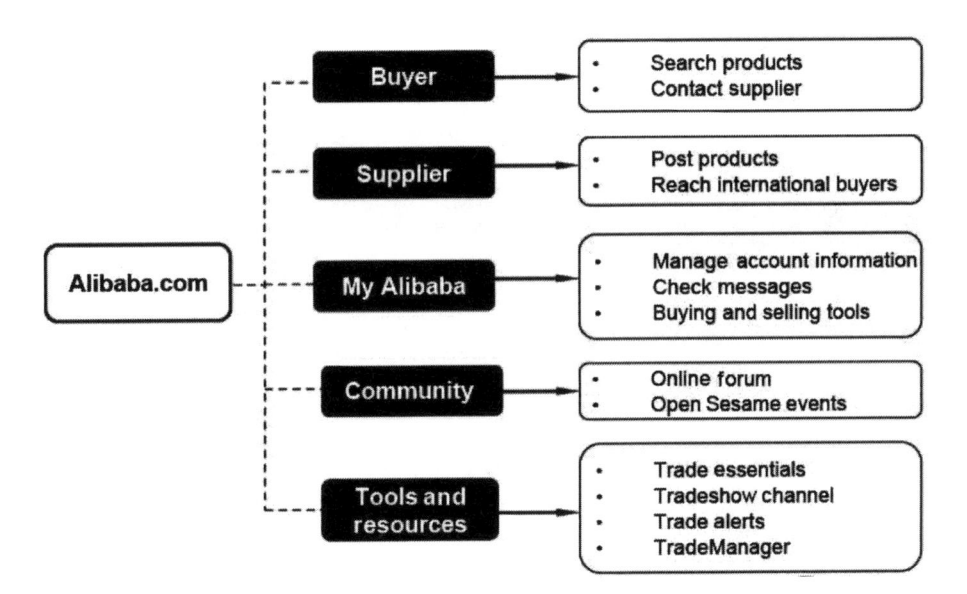

Figure 5.6   AliBaba's approach and tools for innovation (Source: http://www. jteall.com/Alibaba%2001.pdf)

The mission of AliBaba is well aligned with the external and internal environment. It stresses the significance of customers, team work, change, passion and commitment as illustrated in Figure 5.7.

Customer first	The interests of our community of users and paying members must be our first priority.
Team work	We expect our employees to collaborate as a team. We encourage input from our employees in the decision-making process, and expect every employee to commit to the team's objectives.
Embrace change	We operate in a fast-evolving industry. We ask our employees to maintain flexibility, continue to innovate and adapt to new business conditions and practice.
Passion	Our employees are encouraged to act with passion whether it is serving customers or developing new services and products.
Commitment	Our employees have a dedicated focus and commitment to understanding and delivering on the needs of Chinese and global SMEs.

Figure 5.7 **AliBaba's mission and values as a global e-business organization (Source: http://www.jteall.com/Alibaba%2001.pdf)**

In sum, the innovation process is underpinned by the business model since it is simply about creating value to users and addressing a market need. However, technology policy and public policy play a key role in addressing market failures and aligning technology and innovation policy with national development policy. The following is a set of case studies on various types of innovation.

5.4 CASE STUDY 5.1: THE AGU IN BAHRAIN AS A MODEL FOR REGIONAL INTEGRATION

The formation of the GCC in the 1980s was an initiative to consolidate and articulate a new vision for the oil-producing countries in the Arabian Gulf region. The GCC includes the Kingdom of Saudi Arabia (KSA), Kuwait, the UAE, Qatar, Bahrain and Oman. The rational imperative for the GCC was underpinned by economic, social and environmental realities, which highlights the basic notion that the whole is greater than the sum of the parts. Regional integration was the cornerstone for the GCC's harnessing of synergies and evolution of joint initiatives in business, development and defence.

High-quality university education is essential for transforming societies into knowledge economies. Hence, investing in human, intellectual and institutional capital is crucial to providing the enabling environment for innovation and prosperity. The AGU in Bahrain is determined to become a leader in academic education and R&D by addressing the development issues of the GCC countries. The AGU is keen to harness and utilize its core competences in R&D and unique academic programmes to gain an eminent international reputation.

The vision of the AGU is to become one of the leading academic innovation hubs in the GCC, by providing transformative education that contributes to sustainable development. The AGU is keen to address the regional priorities of the GCC, which include health, human development, the environment, science and technology. After three decades of operation, the AGU underwent a salient transformation in the philosophy and strategy of teaching the graduate programme in Innovation and Technology Management (ITM). The ITM programme mandate is to link science, business and technology in the Arabian Gulf. In 2015, the ITM programme focused on green technology, smart cities, climate change, social innovation and open and user innovation.

Since the late 1990s, the centre of gravity for innovation has started to shift from the Levant and North Africa to this part of the world. This shift has been driven by huge investment in construction, infrastructure and technology transfer initiatives, including investment in research and technology in places such as King Abdullah City for Science and Technology (KACST), the AGU, Masdar City, the Qatar Foundation, and King Abdullah University for Science and Technology (KAUST). Since its inception in the early 1980s, the AGU in Bahrain has aimed to be a regional research university addressing the development priorities of the region in collaboration with global partners in medicine, business, technology and education. The AGU played a key role in contributing to the water, energy and food discourse and helping formulate strategies and policies for the GCC and Arab League.

Innovation in the AGU is manifested in many domains including the adoption of personalized medicine, problem-based learning and soilless agriculture. Innovative partnerships with international agencies, the public sector and industry are evident in the design of the programme for natural resources water management with United Nations University, biotechnology, the geographic information system, distance learning programmes, gifted education and special needs education. In addition, the ITM programme offers a platform for research and reflection within industry, the public sector and civil society. The key question is how new disruptive technologies may change the business model of the AGU and GCC in light of Vision 2030 which stresses the significance of the knowledge economy, innovation and economic diversification. The AGU is keen to validate the notion that a regional innovative university can be a catalyst for shaping and forming an innovative region in the GCC.

Source: Arabian Gulf University website.
Available online at http://www.agu.edu.bh/Default_en.aspx [Accessed 24 September 2015].

5.5 CASE STUDY 5.2: TALABAT.COM – THE FIRST ONLINE BUSINESS IN KUWAIT

E-business revolutionized the conventional model of service delivery worldwide after the World Wide Web was invented in the early 1990s. The web-based platforms opened new possibilities and opportunities for innovations in business models. A good example from Kuwait is the delivery of food online via Talabat.com, the first online business in the GCC with a network of over 1,400 restaurants (www.talabat. com). Innovation is simply about connecting the dots and generating an idea that can add value and generate a profit. In 2004, Talabat.com was established with a budget of about $1,000 serving only 200 customers, based on an idea by a Kuwaiti entrepreneur who saw an opportunity and a market demand for providing food online. By 2007, its worth was about one million dollars.

Due to a rise in demand to around 1,600 customers, and confidence in the quality of the service, the firm was sold in 2010 for about 2 million dollars. In 2015, Talabat.com was serving 50,000 customers and its worth was about 150 million euros. Talabat. com is a success story from the GCC which highlights that risk taking, entrepreneurship and imagination pay off.

Source: Talabat.com website.
Available online at https://www.talabat.com/uae [Accessed 21January 2016]

5.6 CASE STUDY 5.3: THE NATIONAL CAR – MALAYSIA AND EGYPT

Historically, Egypt represented a hub for cultural exchange and an interface with other civilizations. In the eleventh century Napoleon introduced printing and contributed to promoting a process of technology transfer from Europe. In the eighteenth century, during the Ottoman Empire, the local governor, Mohammad Ali, initiated a modernization process and institutional reform through modern education and technology transfer.

After the end of the King Farouq Era, in the early twentieth century, a new regime in 1952 started a nationalization process with an emphasis on industrialization. As a result, an initiative for manufacturing a national car called Naser started in 1960. The trajectory of the life cycle of the national car in Egypt was pioneering and very promising thanks to government protection and subsidies. However, the open market and a liberalization policy in the 1990s resulted in a decline in the technology S-curve. Eventually, in 2009, the government decided to end the production of the Naser car.

In contrast, Malaysia launched a national car called Proton in 1983. This was part of Mahatir Mohammad's vision to raise the profile and visibility of Malaysia. The transition of Malaysia from an agricultural economy based on rubber and palm oil to a knowledge and technological innovation economy was a transformative journey. The S-curve of the Malaysian national car, Proton, underwent the pioneering and growth stages during the 1980s and took about 60 per cent of the domestic market share. In the 1990s, the national car experienced a decline in sales due to the economic slowdown. However, the auto industry in Malaysia adopted a new strategy and expanded into the UK market in the early 1990s to ensure a sustainable business model. It is illuminating to track and map the S-curve for the two national cars and develop a deeper understanding of the rise and fall of national industries and learn from global experiences.

The narrative and evolution of the two cases of national cars in Egypt and Malaysia shed light on the necessary and sufficient conditions for the success of a national strategic industry. These include:

- Alignment of development plans with technology and innovation policy;

- The harnessing of global alliances and partnerships for technology acquisition and diffusion;

- Investment in R&D to ensure continuous improvement;

- Provision of an enabling environment for innovation.

Source: Ahram Online. Egypt plans to reoperate the legendary Nasr car production company. Available online at http://english.ahram.org.eg/NewsContent/3/12/64462/Business/ Economy/Egypt-plans-to-reoperate-the-legendary-Nasr-car-pr.aspx [Accessed October 2015].

5.7 CASE STUDY 5.4: MASDAR CITY – A LOW-CARBON CITY IN THE UAE

The global climate change conference in 2015 in Paris defined a global agenda and mandate to make a make a transition to a low-carbon economy. MENA and GCC countries are taking steps to diversify their economies and mainstream eco-solutions and practices. Such a transition to sustainability implies a shift to a new business model including changes in the energy mix and governance of the energy sector.

GCC countries, such as the UAE, Bahrain, Oman, Kuwait, Qatar and Saudi Arabia, have developed a number of initiatives to make a transition to renewable energy. This move is likely to introduce new paradigms in development that are characterized by decentralized modes of energy delivery like Feed-in-Tariff and new roles for the private sector (Al-Jayyousi, 2015). The model of Masdar City in the UAE is a testimony to the adoption and diffusion of clean technology.

Masdar City (http://www.masdar.ae/) in Abu Dhabi, UAE is a model for a green city or low-carbon initiative to present a business case for the green economy. Masdar was initiated in 2006 during a rise in oil prices to reduce the ecological footprint in the UAE and to showcase a global model for a sustainable city in an oil-producing country. The city is being built with 54 acres of solar panels, together with energy and water efficiency systems. The city hosts the Masdar Institute for Higher Education in Sustainability Studies.

In essence, the resilience and sustainability of cities depends on the ability to balance the economic, social and ecological components. GCC countries, and other countries in the Arab world, need to adopt an ecological modernization model by mainstreaming the environment in the economy. The necessary conditions for transforming the GCC countries into an innovative region include a transformation of city governance, aligning education to the regional vision, building a knowledge base for best practices and strategic alliances in STI and green energy.

The enablers for a transition to a green and smart city include quality education and good governance of institutions. Learning organizations are the cornerstone for establishing such a green, smart city. To facilitate the transition, learning organizations require key characteristics including having a shared vision and system thinking. Key institutions, including the International Agency of Renewable Energy, Masdar City, the Qatar Foundation in Qatar and King Abdulla City for Science and Technology in the KSA, provide a hub for sustainable innovation. Green initiatives present vivid evidence of the relevance of and need for a green economy. The trend for green cities, green buildings, green SMEs, green technology, green industry and green infrastructure is shaping a new paradigm of green development.

In sum, the implications for such a transition are compelling in terms of the developmental models in the GCC, consumption patterns, green SMEs, green technology and cleaner production. Moreover, a transition to a low-carbon economy in the GCC is associated with knowledge creation and new governance of natural resources. This shift is likely to have deep implications in terms of innovation policy, green construction and the role of the private sector in renewable energy. The key question is whether the Masdar model can be sustainable when the oil prices rise to levels that make renewable energy economically unfeasible.

Source: Al-Jayyousi, Odeh Rashed (2015). Renewable Energy in the Arab World: Transfer of Knowledge and Prospects of Arab Cooperation. Amman, Jordan: FES. Available online at http://library.fes.de/pdf-files/bueros/amman/11667.pdf [Accessed October 2016].

References and related bibliography

Al-Jayyousi, O. R. (2015). *Renewable Energy in the Arab World: Transfer of Knowledge and Prospects for Arab Cooperation*, Amman: FES.

Boons, F., Montalvo, C., Quist, J. and Wagner, M. (2013). Sustainable innovation, business models and economic performance: an overview. *Journal of Cleaner Production*, 45, 1–8.

Curley, M. and Salmelin, B. (2013). *Open Innovation 2.0: A New Paradigm*. Cambridge, MA: Academic Press.

Keeley, L., Walters, H., Pikkel, R. and Quinn, B. (2013). *Ten Types of Innovation: The Discipline of Building Breakthroughs*. Hoboken, NJ: John Wiley & Sons.

Kline, S. J. and Rosenberg, N. (1986). An overview of innovation. *The Positive Sum Strategy: Harnessing Technology for Economic Growth*, 14, 640.

Osterwalder, A. and Pigneur, Y. (2010). *Business Model Generation: A Handbook for Visionaries, Game Changers, and Challengers*. Hoboken, NJ: John Wiley & Sons. Also available online at https://www.intec.edu.do/downloads/pdf/vriv/emprendurismo-innovacion/recursos/business-model-generation-a-handbook-for-visionaries-game-changers-and-challengers.pdf [Accessed 20 June 2016].

Pavitt, K. (1984). Sectoral patterns of technical change: towards a taxonomy and a theory. *Research Policy*, 13(6), 343–373.

Schumpeter, J. A. (1939). *Business Cycles*, (Vol. 1). New York: McGraw-Hill, pp. 161–174.

Urban, G. L. and Von Hippel, E. (1988). Lead user analyses for the development of new industrial products. *Management Science*, 34(5), 569–582.

Winter, S. G. and Nelson, R. R. (1982). An evolutionary theory of economic change. *University of Illinois at Urbana-Champaign's Academy for Entrepreneurial Leadership Historical Research Reference in Entrepreneurship*. Cambridge, MA: Belknap Press.

6

Individual innovation

The crisis in the MENA region and the Muslim world at large is the absence of enablers for innovation; the future lies in the investment in genuine integral innovation.

(The author)

This chapter aims at achieving the following objectives:

- Identify and define the role of individual traits and characteristics in innovation;

- Discuss system thinking for individual innovation;

- Explain the factors that promote and inhibit individual innovation.

The model of integral innovation consists of a set of enablers as depicted in (ICON). This chapter addresses the Individual innovation as the first element in the integral innovation model as illustrated in Figure 6.1.

In assessing the continuity or discontinuity points in the ICON model, it seems to me that, in many cases, the seeds of innovations that are nurtured at the individual and community/city level are not harnessed, made to flourish or enhanced at either the organizational or the national level. The innovation climate and culture of the home and neighbourhood are disrupted at the organizational and national level. This issue is critical for sustaining and scaling up the momentum and impulse of innovation to develop an innovative nation.

Moreover, it is interesting to note that in the integral innovation model technical and economic innovation are not properly informed or reformed by cultural and ecological innovations. As a result, the systemic and structural challenges in many

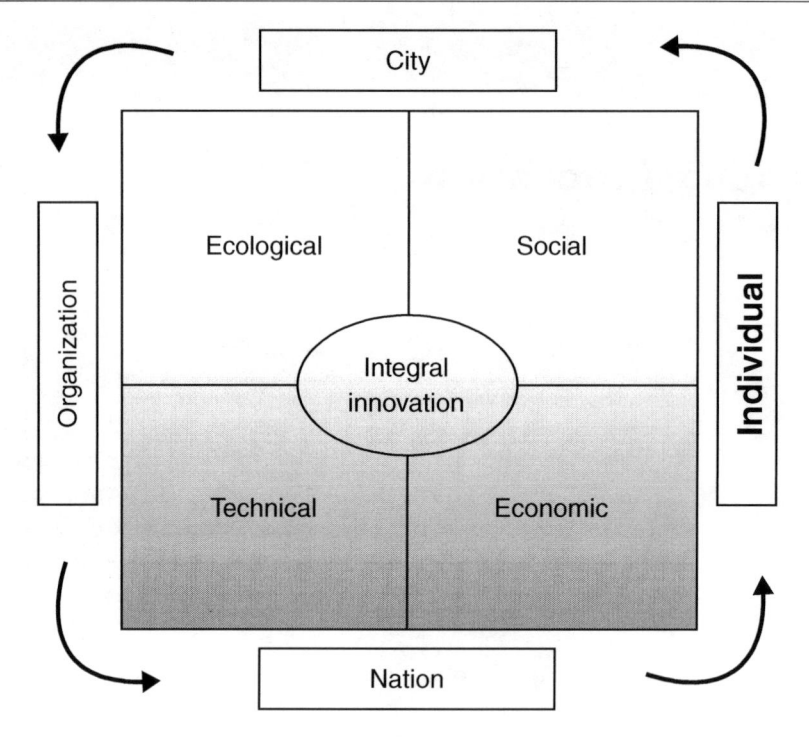

Figure 6.1   A model for integral innovation focusing on individual innovation

of the countries in transition may be explained by two "breakdowns" in the integral innovation model.

Human creativity and innovation underpin organizational and social innovation. Identification of key traits and behaviours of innovative people is crucial to managing talent in organizations. The key questions are how we can harness the potential of innovative individuals in an organization and how organizational cultures and climates can support individual innovation.

6.1 Individual innovation

There is a divergence of opinions with respect to the role of individuals in organizational innovation. However, there are strong proponents for the view that individual leadership plays a key role in organizational innovation, as argued by Gehani (2011). This concern is a critical national issue since unlocking human potential is a driver for national prosperity and economic growth. Research in applied psychology and behavioural sciences shows key traits and features of innovative people. These include a desire for autonomy, social independence, tolerance for ambiguity and tendency for risk taking.

Individual innovation is informed by both cultural and organizational settings. The success and resilience of organizations is underpinned by sustainable innovation (Lyon and Ferrier, 2002). The imperative of organizational innovations to sustain relevance and competitiveness was introduced by Schumpeter in the early 1930s (Schumpeter, 1934). However, open and user innovation was introduced by Hippel in the 1980s and demonstrated that the public at large and users are key sources for innovation. This chapter intends to explore the key factors for enhancing individual innovation which is part of ICON innovation. One of the fundamental issues is how to unlock the individual innovations and harness them to the community, organization and nation. The paradox of many developing nations is the fact that the intensity of innovation is reduced and diluted as we move through the ICON domains. The resilience of the sustainability-innovation nexus is maintained if the intensity increases as we move across the four elements of ICON.

In a globalized market economy, harnessing innovation is the key to enhancing productivity and achieving competitiveness. The notions of creativity, inventions and innovations are founded on individual assets that are harnessed and unlocked through an innovative climate, culture and process. The virtual world and the global market place have induced and formed new platforms and institutions like eBay, Amazon, Uber and Airbnb which require new innovative human talent, organizational structure and governance. The capacity of an organization to manage knowledge is defined as its *absorptive capacity* which is considered vital for enabling innovation to become global. Mahroum (2008) argues that a key to sustaining the intensity of innovation is to go global.

Intellectual and human capitals are essential for transforming organizations and nations. The key asset of an organization is the human capital since "people, not products, are an innovative company's major assets" (Gupta and Singhal, 1993). Leadership and human resource development are crucial for supporting a culture and climate for innovation. The notion of individual innovation is about transforming human creativity into sustained and implementable products, process and systems. Individual innovation is shaped and framed by external factors like education, the market and national policies. Education plays a pivotal role in shaping the landscape and ecosystem for innovation (Dakhli and de Clercq, 2004).

The new discoveries in genomes, genetic engineering and brain research inform new ideas about individual innovation being linked to genetics and the external environment. A set of distinct features were identified for an innovative individual:

1. Intellectual capital;

2. Specialized and generalized knowledge;

3. Modes and styles of thinking;

4. Personality traits;

5. Motivation.

The likelihood or propensity to innovate is associated with the above five factors as defined by Sternberg and Lubart (1999). In addition, they stated that individual innovation is related to human cognitive ability, knowledge, personality, behaviour and motivation.

There is a general consensus that knowledge, skills and motivation are the key to individual innovation. Having a focused and specialized knowledge in a specific domain is a necessary, but not sufficient, condition for innovation. However, diverse and interdisciplinary knowledge is likely to enhance the likelihood of innovation (Sternberg, 1982). Innovators are highly motivated and have a high level of absorption in their work (Eysenck, 1994). In exploring environmental influences on motivation, there are developmental factors, external factors and resources within an organization to be considered, as illustrated in Figure 6.2.

There is a relationship between innovation and *personality*. An innovative personality is characterized as being imaginative, inquisitive and highly self-confident. The five-factor model of personality may be insightful for studying innovation. The factors are:

1. Openness to experience;

2. Agreeableness;

3. Conscientiousness;

4. Extroversion;

5. Neuroticism.

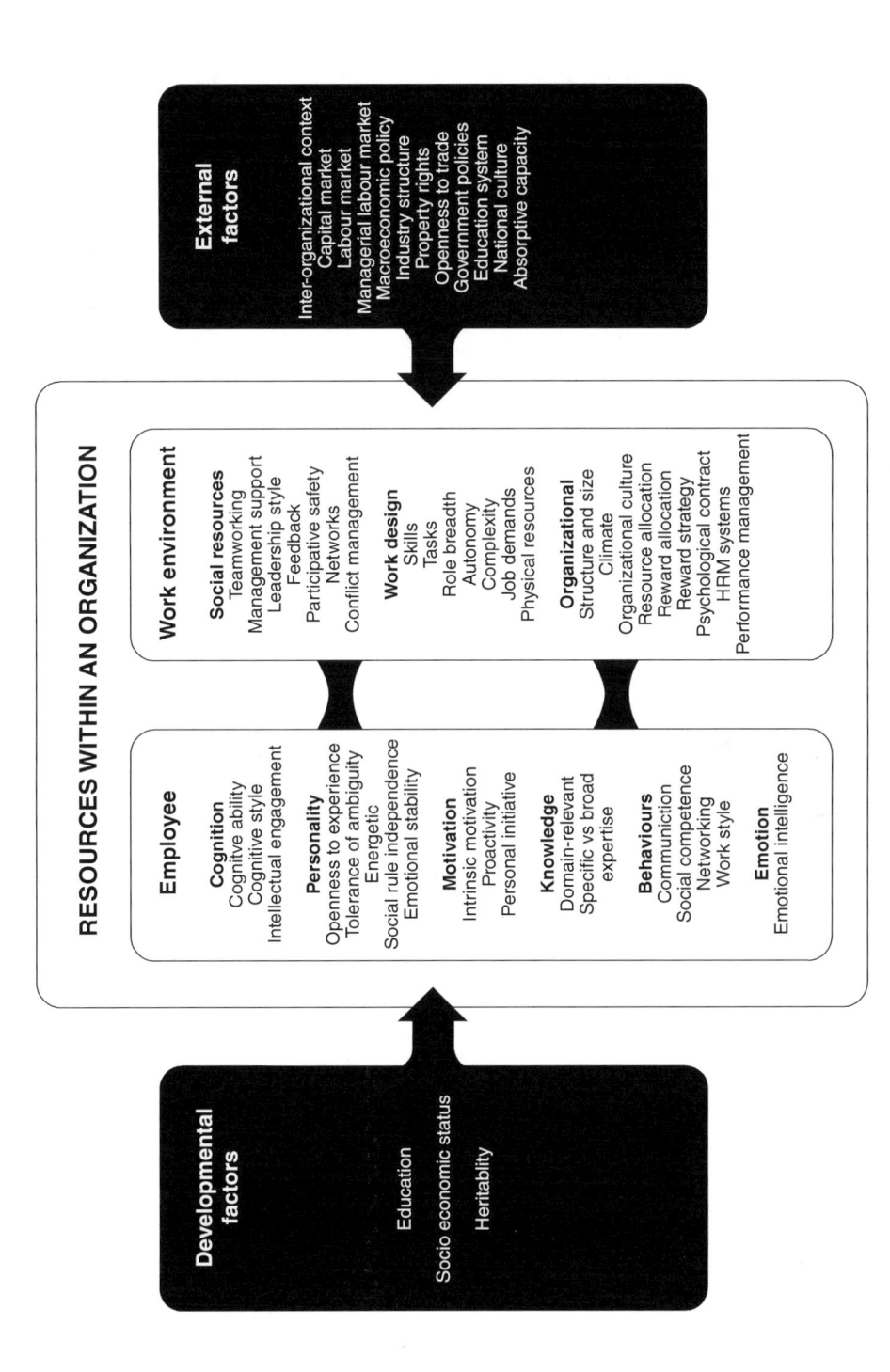

Figure 6.2   Resource assets for individual innovations in organizations (Source: Patterson, Kerrin and Gatto-Roissard, 2009)

In terms of identifying the *behaviour* of innovative people, the concept of personal initiative (PI) describes key characteristics and conditions that underpin innovation. PI is correlated with risk taking and perseverance which is essential at the initiation stage of idea development and the implementation stage in the innovation journey. In addition, the concept of emotional intelligence, which measures the human ability to understand people's feelings and emotions, is key to enabling both individual and organizational innovation as argued by Salovey (1997).

The family environment plays a key role in nurturing and enhancing individual innovation especially at the stage of initiation of new ideas. Mumford, et al. (2002) found that innovation is associated with an enabling environment which includes, education, family environment, adequate culture, norms, values and visible role models. In addition, having an active community/city at an early stage and a supportive *work environment* enhance the propensity for innovation. In principle, individual innovation is augmented by a dynamic and responsive organization that has the ability "to explore new ideas and at the same time harness existing assets which in turn will enhance organizational capacity to *simultaneously pursue both incremental and discontinuous innovation*" (Tushman and O'Reilly, 1996; p. 24).

Transforming an organization into an innovative one requires leadership that is able to embody and instil a culture of trust and team spirit as articulated by Gibson and Birkinshaw (2004). Leadership is a key to fostering and sustaining innovation. Necessary skills for innovative leaders include risk taking, effective communication and delegation of authority. Moreover, using the metaphor of species and ecosystems, individuals (species) require the right habitat (ecosystem/organization) to develop an innovative system. This system is empowered by teams and groups that embody diversity and learning. Specifically, the following are some core values for innovative teams:

- *Operating principles:* Organic and decentralized teams tend to be more adaptive, responsive and innovative, unlike the mechanistic ones, as documented by King and Anderson (2002). Having consensus among the team on operating principles and a code of conduct help foster a climate of innovation.

- *Diversity:* Having diverse teams in terms of education, skills and culture offers rich opportunities for potential innovations and idea generation as concluded by Watson, Kumar and Michaelsen (1993). Also, an organization can tap into the wide array of talents and skills to be harnessed in the innovation process which includes problem identification, idea generation, exploration and implementation, as illustrated in Figure 6.3.

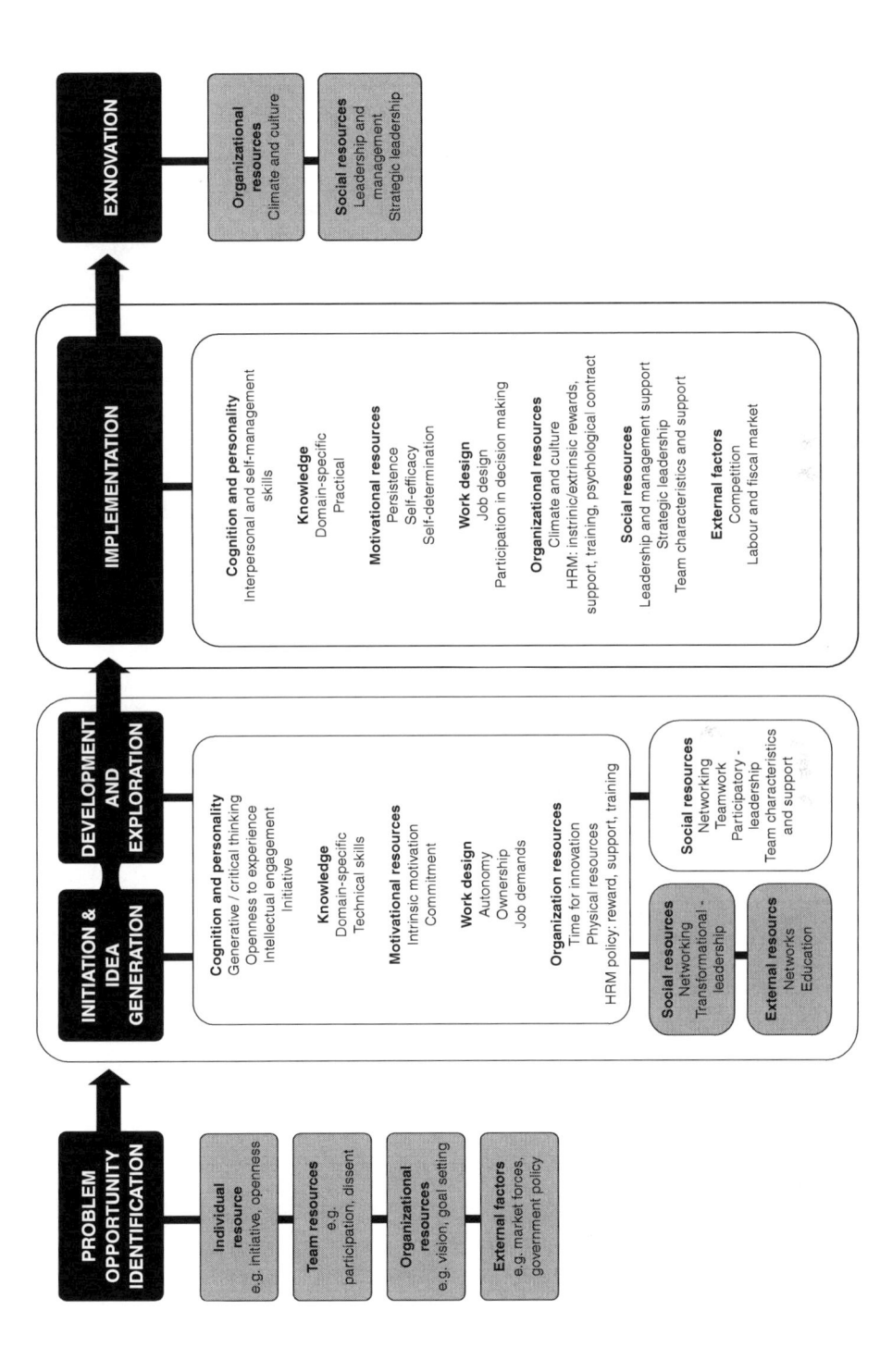

Figure 6.3   Characteristics, behaviours and influencing factors mapped to the innovation process (Source: Patterson, Kerrin and Gatto-Roissard, 2009)

Moreover, a complex variety of factors contribute to enhancing innovation. These include social networks, job complexity and physical settings, as documented by (Shalley, Zhou and Oldham, 2004).

ORGANIZATIONAL CULTURE

The corporate governance and organizational structure shape and influence the climate and culture of innovation. Three factors define the propensity for an organization to innovate. These include centralization, formalization and complexity. There is empirical evidence that centralized structures limit the potential for organizational innovation as articulated by Burns and Stalker (1961). In contrast, decentralized structures tend to foster innovation since this supports group decision making and accountability. On the other hand, high formalization limits possibilities of innovation due to institutional inertia and standard procedures. *Complexity* is likely to motivate idea generation and creativity in the organization. In terms of organizational longevity, it seems that SMEs are more likely to have innovative capacity (West and Richter, 2008). Amabile and colleagues (2005) noted that reward and incentive systems are critical for fostering innovation. Other factors that spur innovation include (a) *celebrating failure and valuing new ideas*; (b) *collaborative problem solving*; and (c) *risk taking*.

6.2 Innovation processes in organizations

During the 1990s, Andrew Van de Ven and colleagues studied the innovation process in organizations and concluded that the process is characterized as a *non-linear dynamic system*. King (1992) showed that sequential, linear models were most applicable for *incremental* innovations. King and Anderson (2002) highlight the concept of "exnovation" which refers to the tendency for organizations to abandon current practice for a new innovation.

Anderson and Gasteiger (2007) argue that in order to fully harness innovation, organizations should focus on specific areas to maximize innovative capacity. It should be noted that it is important to incorporate insights from individuals and teams to inform organizational innovation. However, managers should be aware of possible spillover or disruptive effects of innovation. It is imperative for innovative organizations to invest in human capital to sustain an *innovative culture* which nurtures creativity, learning and risk taking.

The following is a case study that illustrates the model of individual innovation.

6.3 CASE STUDY 6.1: TALAL ABU-GHAZALEH ORGANIZATION

Talal Abu-Ghazaleh is a Palestinian refugee who moved to Lebanon at the age of ten after the 1948 war. He had to leave his homeland and his family business in Jaffa. Talal went to the University of Beirut Business School in the late 1950s and graduated in 1960. He worked as an accountant for few years in Kuwait, started his accounting firm in the mid-1960s, and expanded his business in the 1970s. He established a global firm called the Talal Abu-Ghazaleh Organization (TAG) (www.tagorg.com). The TAG organization now employs about 2,000 professionals and has 86 branches and offices across the globe, in Asia, Europe, Africa and the USA. The core business of TAG includes audits, consultancy, information technology, capacity building, intellectual property and education services.

His personal journey was one of hardship and perseverance. His mottos in life are that success requires:

- Diligence and excellence;

- Global partnerships;

- Ethical and value-based organizations;

- Commitment to community development.

Talal Abu-Ghazaleh's individual innovation journey has been shaped by his hard experiences as a refugee in Lebanon and as a junior employee in Kuwait. The family values instilled in him the value of learning and hard work from an early age. Abu Ghazaleh's strong leadership and ethical code of conduct was inspired by his personal journey, education and family values.

Source:TAG-ORG: The Global Organization for Professional Services and Education.
Available online at http://www.tagorg.com/?lang=en# [Accessed 12 August 2015].

References and related bibliography

Amabile, T. M., Barsade, S. G., Mueller, J. S. and Staw, B. M. (2005). Affect and creativity at work. *Administrative Science Quarterly*, 50(3), 367–403.

Anderson, N. and Gasteiger, R. M. (2007). Helping creativity and innovation thrive in organizations: functional and dysfunctional perspectives. *Research companion to the dysfunctional workplace: Management challenges and symptoms*, 24, 422.

Burns, T. E. and Stalker, G. M. (1961). *The Management of Innovation*. Champaign, IL: University of Illinois at Urbana-Champaign's Academy for Entrepreneurial Leadership Historical Research Reference in Entrepreneurship.

Dakhli, M. and de Clercq, D. (2004). Human capital, social capital, and innovation: a multi-country study. *Entrepreneurship & Regional Development*, 16(2), 107–128.

Eysenck, H. J. (1994). *The Measurement of Creativity*. Cambridge, MA: The MIT Press.

Gehani, R. (2011). Individual creativity and the influence of mindful leaders on enterprise innovation. *Journal of Technology Management & Innovation*, 6(3), 82–92.

Gibson, C. B. and Birkinshaw, J. (2004). The antecedents, consequences, and mediating role of organizational ambidexterity. *Academy of Management Journal*, 47(2), 209–226.

Gupta, A. K. and Singhal, A. (1993). Managing human resources for innovation and creativity. *Research-Technology Management*, 36(3), 41–48.

Janssen, O., Van de Vliert, E. and West, M. (2004). The bright and dark sides of individual and group innovation: A special issue introduction. *Journal of Organizational Behavior*, 25(2), 129–145.

King, N. (1992). Modelling the innovation process: an empirical comparison of approaches. *Journal of Occupational and Organizational Psychology*, 65(2), 89–100.

King, N. and Anderson, N. (2002). *Managing Innovation and Change: A Critical Guide for Organizations*. London: Cengage Learning EMEA.

Lyon, D. W. and Ferrier, W. J. (2002). Enhancing performance with product-market innovation: the influence of the top management team. *Journal of Managerial Issues*, 14(4), 452–469.

Mahroum, S. (2008). *Innovation by Adoption: Measuring and Mapping Absorptive Capacity in UK Nations and Regions*. London: Nesta.

Mayer, J. D., Caruso, D. R. and Salovey, P. (1999). Emotional intelligence meets traditional standards for an intelligence. *Intelligence*, 27(4), 267–298.

Mumford, M. D., Scott, G. M., Gaddis, B. and Strange, J. M. (2002). Leading creative people: Orchestrating expertise and relationships. *The Leadership Quarterly*, 13(6), 705–750.

Patterson, F., Kerrin, M. and Gatto-Roissard, G. (2009). *Characteristics and Behaviours of Innovative People in Organisations: Literature Review*. A paper prepared for the NESTA Policy & Research Unit, London: City University, pp. 1–63.

Salovey, P. (1997). *Emotional Development and Emotional Intelligence: Educational Implications*. New York: Basic Books.

Schumpeter, J. A. (1934). *The Theory of Economic Development: An Inquiry into Profits, Capital, Credit, Interest, and the Business Cycle* (Vol. 55). New Brunswick, NJ: Transaction Publishers.

Shalley, C. E., Zhou, J. and Oldham, G. R. (2004). The effects of personal and contextual characteristics on creativity: where should we go from here? *Journal of Management*, 30(6), 933–958.

Sternberg, R. J. (1982). *Handbook of Human Intelligence*. Cambridge: Cambridge University Press.

Sternberg, R. (1990). The impact of innovation centres on small technology-based firms: The example of the Federal Republic of Germany. *Small Business Economics*, 2(2), 105–118.

Sternberg, R. J. and Lubart, T. I. (1999). The concept of creativity: Prospects and paradigms. *Handbook of Creativity*, 1, 3–15.

Tushman, M. L. and O'Reilly, C. A. (1996). The ambidextrous organizations: Managing evolutionary and revolutionary change. *California Management Review*, 38(4), 8–30.

Van de Ven, A. H. and Poole, M. S. (1990). Methods for studying innovation development in the Minnesota Innovation Research Program. *Organization Science*, 1(3), 313–335.

Van de Ven, A. H., Polley, D. and Garud, R. (2008). *The Innovation Journey*. New York: Oxford University Press.

Watson, W. E., Kumar, K. and Michaelsen, L. K. (1993). Cultural diversity's impact on interaction process and performance: Comparing homogeneous and diverse task groups. *Academy of Management Journal*, 36(3), 590–602.

West, M. A. and Anderson, N. R. (1996). Innovation in top management teams. *Journal of Applied Psychology*, 81(6), 680.

West, M. A. and Richter, A. (2008). Climates and cultures for innovation and creativity at work. In: J. Zhou and C. E. Shalley (eds), *Handbook of Organizational Creativity*. New York: Lawrence Erlbaum Associates, pp. 211–236.

7

Innovative communities and cities

What makes the City of Boston an innovative hub for education and health care is its ability to attract talent from the global market.

(The author)

7.1 Overview

In summer 2016, during my visit to the City of Boston to attend a conference at Harvard Business School on Open and User Innovation, it was illuminating to realize how innovative cities like Boston invested in their infrastructure to add value and create knowledge. The history of Boston as explained in the Duck Tour is a story of war and triumph against all odds. In September every year, Boston attracts about 300,000 students to be educated in two of the finest institutions of the world: Harvard and MIT.

This chapter highlights the role of cities/communities as interactive laboratories of innovation. The innovative city is underpinned by organizational, cultural and social innovation as illustrated in the integral innovation model in Figure 7.1. The first section discusses a theoretical and conceptual framework for creative cities. The second section presents the conditions and reasons for the collapse (or creative destruction) of innovative cities by illustrating the current conditions of these cities in the twenty-first century. The third part presents a conceptual foundation for the reconstruction of innovative cities by looking at the three phases of *creation, destruction* and *reconstruction*.

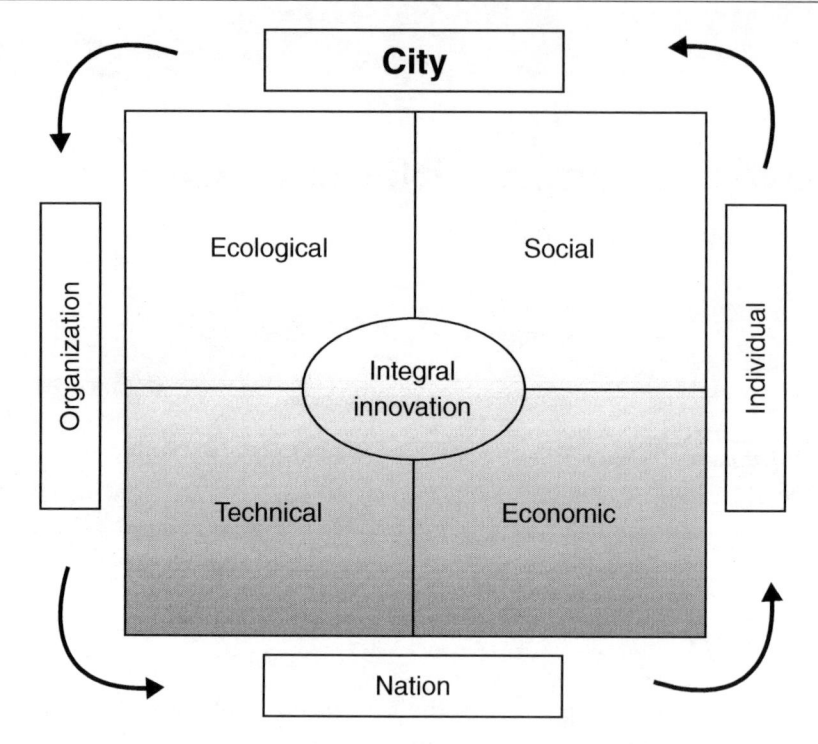

Figure 7.1   **A model for integral innovation focusing in community/city innovation**

7.2 Creative cities: theoretical framework

Viewing the city as an interactive laboratory for innovation is an inspiring business model for a sustainable and smart city. Hahn (2010) argued that defining the concepts of "creative city" (Landry, 2008) and "creative class" (Florida, 2002) highlighted the importance of social capital and culture in the meaning and value of urban space. The creative city concept has become a characteristic in urban planning due to changes in the labour force and a shift to a knowledge and service economy. A creative community or city provides the ecosystem and enabling environment for nurturing and celebrating a culture of diversity and openness.

As individuals, initial innovative and creative journeys are experienced at home and in the local neighbourhood but after graduating from university and starting professional careers, many innovative individuals are constrained within organizational and national systems that limit space for innovations. The key question is how to transform our organizations and NISs to unlock, nurture and enhance the capacity and culture of innovation. Moreover, the innovation journey will be more fruitful and resilient if it is founded on both cultural and ecological innovations and is able to manage change in all seasons. Innovation in all *four seasons* is crucial for the transformation of ICON. The creation, destruction, and reconstruction of an innovative city is a story of the human pursuit of progress and prosperity in a journey that is constrained and defined by resources, human capital and external factors.

Realizing and revitalizing the notion of culture as a creative asset is stressed in the work of Landry (2008) when he asserts the importance of culture as a creative resource. Every individual is a potential source of production of creative products and processes which is part of both social and political innovation. In addition, the value of space is vital for cross-fertilization, social cohesion and interaction. Florida (2002) stressed the idea that "place is the key economic and social organizing unit of our time" since it creates a sense of meaning and purpose for people, the environment and the economy. Establishing an enabling ecosystem for innovative communities is crucial for sustainable and smart cities. The city is no longer solely a "functional" space with a separation between life and work and standardized forms of consumption and leisure, as in the functional city (Reckwitz, 2002). On the contrary, the "creative" city is viewed as a cultural figure with identity and meaning. The following section is based on my book, *Islam and Sustainable Development: New Worldviews* (Al-Jayyousi, 2016).

Within the creative city model the presence and concentration of artists and scientists are linked to the city's economic development because these groups foster creativity and appeal to the new class. Different instruments for measuring innovation in cities were developed like the "creativity index", "3Ts" (technology, talent and tolerance) and "urban innovation matrix" (Florida, 2002).

A community of practice with both scientists and artists is likely to form a creative class that has a mission to develop an innovative space and culture. This community of talented human capital creates a value through the fusion of ideas and images that shape the identity of a city. The city becomes more adaptive and responsive to the economic, communal and ecological needs of a creative community of practice. An innovative city is the common space that celebrates the co-existence of human talent and imagination to make a new meaning of space.

A city resembles an ecosystem that is formed from a web of connections to develop a "sustainable human community" that is founded on the notions and principles of ecology which include creativity, learning, networks, cycles, partnership and diversity (Capra, 1996). The following sections outline the three phases of evolution of innovative cities – creation, destruction and reconstruction – in light of the evolution of Islamic cities and the current state of key cities in the MENA region including Baghdad, Damascus and Cairo.

7.3 The creation of innovative cities: the Islamic city as a model for innovation

The emergence of Islamic cities like Damascus, Jerusalem, Baghdad and Cairo was centred around education centres and mosques. The urban culture is clearly manifested in Islamic civilization. This was evident in the early formation of the Islamic city which was established around the mosque in Medina. As documented by Afsaruddin (2005) and Al-Jayyousi (2016), during Prophet Mohammad's time, the mosque in Medina served both as the locus of private and public worship and as the centre for informal instruction of the believers in religious law and related matters. The mosque continued to play these multiple roles throughout the first three centuries of Islam (the seventh, eighth and ninth centuries of the Christian or the Common Era). By the tenth century, a new feature, a hostel (*khan*) was increasingly being established next to "teaching mosques" in Iraq and the eastern provinces of the Islamic world which allowed students and teachers from far-flung areas to reside near these places of instruction. The emergence of the mosque-*khan* complex at this time is a consequence of the lengthier and more intensive period of study required to qualify as a religious scholar.

In the tenth and eleventh centuries of the Common Era, another important institution known as the *madrasa*, literally meaning "a place of study", developed and proliferated. One of the Fatimid's enduring intellectual legacies was the establishment of the oldest continuing university in the world – the al-Azhar mosque-*madrasa* complex in Cairo – in 972 CE. Perhaps the most prominent name associated with the spread of *madrasas* particularly in Iraq was Nizam al-Mulk (d. 1092), the Saljuq minister. His name is associated with the well-known Nizamiyya academy in Baghdad, famous for scholars like Abu Hamid as-Ghazali (d.1111).

Henceforth, the *madrasa* became the principal venue and vehicle for the transmission of religious education in the major urban centres of the Islamic world, such as Baghdad, Cairo, Damascus and Jerusalem. It was the institution of higher learning comparable to a modern college, for which it was the precursor. In addition to mosques, mosque-*khans*, and *madrasas*, other institutions developed over time which played important, supplementary roles in the dissemination of learning. One of the most significant institutions of this type was the library, burgeoning from the ninth century on. The larger mosques often had libraries attached to them containing books on religious topics. Other semi-public libraries would additionally have books on logic, philosophy, music, astronomy, geometry, medicine, astronomy and chemistry. The first academy in the Islamic world, known in Arabic as *Bayt Al-hikma* (House of Wisdom), was built by the Abbasid caliph al-Ma'mun (813–833), and had a library and an astronomical observatory attached to it.

According to Afsaruddin (2005), the *madrasa* was typically funded by a trust fund (*waqf*), a charitable foundation, a form of institutional organization that was borrowed by the West from the Islamic world towards the end of the eleventh century. *Waqf* rendered a person's property safe from confiscation by the state by freezing it as a public asset which could, however, be passed on to the founder's descendants. In relation to the Quran and Hadith, learning by heart (*talqin*) was the principal method of acquiring knowledge and a retentive memory was, therefore, greatly prized.

The saying "learning is a city, one of its gates is memory and the other is understanding" captures the approach to learning in this era. In the study of law, the scholastic method of disputation (*munathara*) prevailed, a pedagogical method that originated quite early in the Islamic milieu. As early as the middle of the eighth century during the Abbasid period, strong interest began developing in the learning of the ancient world, particularly its Greek sources, but also to a lesser extent its Persian and Indian ones. The intellectual awakening that this interest spawned has rendered this age especially illustrious in the annals of Islamic and world history. Due to the political and territorial expansion of Islam beyond the original Arabian Peninsula, Muslims became the heirs of the older cultures they encountered.

At the time of the Arab conquest of the Fertile Crescent, the intellectual legacy of Greece was unquestionably the most precious treasure at hand. Under the two Abbasid caliphs al-Mahdi and his son Harun-al-Rashid, in particular, the Muslim army won decisive victories over the Byzantine enemy forces. One of the most important achievements of al-Ma'mun's rule is his establishment of the previously mentioned Bayt al-Hikma (the House of Wisdom) in 830. The House of Wisdom was a combination of a library, an academy and a translation bureau. One historian has described the Bayt al-Hikma as the most important educational institution since the foundation of the Alexandrian Museum in the first half of the third century BC. Under al-Ma'mun, the Bayt al-Hikma became the centre of translation activity. This era of avid translation would last through the early tenth century.

The creation of the early model of an innovative city was a result of the confluence of many cultures. Greek, Persian and Indian cultures were assimilated and selectively synthesized with Islamic scholarship. This in turn enriched the innovation in sciences and fostered the cultivation of the natural sciences, philosophy and mathematics.

The construction of the first Islamic city was underpinned by the innovative transformation of the inner beauty to the outer world so as to construct a world (*emartu al ard*) of beauty and excellence in all domains; i.e., individual, organization and society, as documented by Al-Jayyousi (2016). The innovative space from an

Islamic worldview is about instilling a deeper sense of unity, beauty, order and harmony in all domains of life. The following section outlines the conceptual and cultural concepts that form an innovative Islamic city:

1.   *Unity of individual and community: Ihsan* is an Arabic term which has many meanings like excellence and beauty. This also refers to a higher level of evolving consciousness which is above *Islam* (worship of body) and *Iman* (worship of heart). The Arabesque art in its repetition of single elements and shapes illustrates the contribution of an individual element to the whole and to the community. *Ihsan* is about the continuous improvement of the individual within the community and the awareness of the Divine in every act which results in the evolution of an inner beauty and insight. Hence, through this inner renewable consciousness, human actions are regulated to protect the freedom of the community. True individual value and freedom is found in doing what is good and beautiful for the community. The unveiling of beauty in humans, nature and the cosmos provides an inspiration for *ihsan* which is doing what is good and beautiful for the community of life.

2.   *Unity of tradition and modernity:* Islamic art is manifested in landscape, art, architecture and urban design through integrating pre-existing artistic traditions and adapting them to their own scope and demands as reflected in the Dome of the Rock in Jerusalem – the first monument of Islam (688–692) and the Ummayed Great Mosque in Damascus (706–716). In its creative phases, the art of the Muslim world was the product of a new syntax and of a new semantic order for an older visual structure. The City of Jerusalem in the second century as it was during the Islamic rule, where all people had a space and a role to play in a city that embraced "togetherness" and unity within diversity, can be thought of as a model for celebrating ethnic and cultural diversity. It was this deep sense of *ihsan* that inspired Omar bin Khattab (the second Muslim Khalifa after Prophet Mohammed) not to say prayers in the church so as to respect the Christian space.

     For Muslims, Islamic art was not a new invention but an assimilative selection, refinement and recombination of the past and the new and the blending of tradition and modernity. This process, in essence, is a core meaning of the process of excellence and constructed beauty. This selective assimilation was a defining one in creating early Islamic art since the new Muslims needed an aesthetic mode that could satisfy the spiritual aspirations and link them to the roots of Abrahamic monotheism.

3. *Unity of the visible and the invisible:* The key role of Islamic art is to reinforce the awareness of God and the realization of the Hereafter (*Akherah*), and the fusion of the invisible (*batin*) and the visible (*thahir*). The challenge of a transition to sustainability from an Islamic perspective, as with art, is to attempt what the early Muslim scholars achieved, that is to reform and transform old notions, concepts and techniques from all cultures and develop new hybrid models that resonate with local knowledge and culture. If we can restore the state of aesthetic degradation through communicating the notion of *ihsan* to the younger generation, then we are on the right track to achieving a sustainable human civilization.

4. *Unity of localism and globalism:* The global influence of the Islamic civilization across the globe from Spain to the Philippines helped spread the aesthetic unity within diversity through Islamic art and architecture. A hundred and fifty years after the coming of Islam, Islamic art had formed its own language and aesthetics. For example, the Great Mosque of Cordoba (785) in al-Andalus and Ibn Tulun Mosque (879) in Egypt no longer represented phases in a tentative evolution but were, in their own right, unsurpassable masterpieces that set standards for proportions of beauty and harmony. It is interesting to visit the Islamic art museum in Doha, Qatar which was designed by a Chinese artist who wrote that he was inspired by the Ibn Tulun mosque in Egypt.

5. *Unity within diversity in culture, space and time:* One of the key characteristics of Islamic art, around which almost all views meet, is its unity within diversity. This unity is best expressed in Arabic by the doctrine of *tawhid* which means the Oneness of God or Unity of God. Despite the major differences in style and performance that are found in countries ranging from Spain and Morocco to India and Indonesia, one can identify an Islamic character of a city or a piece of art. Despite variations in space and time, the unity of Islamic art was a unique characteristic that is reflected in Islamic landscape and architecture. This unity can be attributed mainly to the core of Islamic worldviews shaped by the Quran and the Arabic language which inspire eco-imagination, eco-analogies, eco-metaphors and eco-images informed by the cosmos, nature and human beings.

6. *Unity of stability and change:* A critical feature of Islamic art is mobility of ideas and people due to trade and pilgrimage (*Hajj*). The mobility of people inside and outside the Islamic Empire enabled artists and artisans to spread artistic ideas across space and time. Extensive commercial

activities within the empire and the journey to Mecca for the *Hajj* from all over the Muslim world caused the widest artistic interaction and made possible the exchange and introduction of artistic ideas and notions of *ihsan*. The key question in the twenty-first century is how Islamic cities in general, and Mecca and Jerusalem in particular, can be the hubs for learning and for reclaiming the meaning of both inner and outer beauty.

7.   *Unity of art and science:* Another feature of Islamic art is the ability to transform the "normal and familiar" into the "extraordinary and exciting". It was evident that Islamic artists were able to transform mundane objects of daily use such as rugs, clothes, lamps, jars and plates into rich and stimulating works of art. For the Muslim artistic conscience, an artefact is in itself an object of art the function of which is both aesthetic and practical. For a traditional Muslim artist, there are no minor and major arts. No boundary exists that separates fine art from applied art. All artistic production demands the same degree of care, planning, creativity, attention and skill. Separating art from handicraft is a modern Western concept which first became evident during the Renaissance Era when art was divorced from spirituality, and only gained ground in the nineteenth century during the Industrial Revolution. In Islam, artist and artisan are one, both are the instruments of God in creating beauty, and none of them is a creator on his own.

In a traditional society, every act the application of which requires skill is called art, so that there is an art of agriculture, architecture, smelting, painting and poetry. When the Industrial Revolution took place, industrial design was unheard of and the daily lives of the masses in the West were totally devoid of aesthetics. Only in the twentieth century did industry recognize the aesthetic value of the utilitarian objects.

8.   *Unity of the beauty in the community of life and the cosmos:* According to Islam, a human is the manifestation of the creation of God (*Allah* in Arabic). Humans have a mandate and a trusteeship (*amanah*) by being the vicegerents of God on earth, trusted to create a harmonious relationship between the cosmos, nature and people. All creation reflects the cosmic beauty, magnificence and intelligence (*ihsan*). From an Islamic worldview, Islamic art is one of the means by which humans can nurture and enhance "aesthetic intelligence" as signs (*ayat*) in all species and the cosmos for deeper learning and reflections from nature and the cosmos.

From the spiritual and ethical point of view, Islamic art originates essentially from the Quranic Message which aims to translate concepts and notions into shapes. This implies that the external message (*thahir*) is complimented by an inner reality (*batin*) that represents the invisible internal essence. The *thahir* underlines the quantitative aspect that is obvious, while the qualitative aspect is the inner beauty or the hidden *batin*. In order to fully realize the complete meaning of beauty and excellence, one must seek to comprehend both types of knowledge, the visible and the invisible, or the software and hardware of things.

9. *Unity of work and worship:* Of specific value, Islamic art belongs to a culture that is characterized by the role of a community and shaped the ideal of becoming liberated from one's self and ego, and where human individuality becomes a means rather than an end. The Islamic worldview is informed by the sayings of the Prophet: "God has inscribed beauty upon all things", "God desires that if you do something you perfect it", "Work is a form of worship" and "God is beautiful and He loves beauty". Hence, perfecting one's artistic work becomes a form of worship and a religious obligation easily fulfilled by the artist through adherence to the faith and its convictions. Islamic artists' key role is to search for new ideas and techniques that could further intensify human fascination with the entirety of life.

It is the combination of reason, intellect, skill and insight that should be harnessed by Muslim artists to project the inner self in a form that reflects the outside reality. Accordingly, all Islamic art is created through a wedding of the formal sciences and the crafts. During the Golden Age of Islam, professionals, artisans and artists followed the Prophet's saying "God desires if you do something you perfect it". This code of conduct ensures quality control, standards, inspiration and continuity. Islamic art should be viewed as a tool that compliments and supports spiritual life. There is evidence that when there is an eclipse of the spiritual life, this will be reflected negatively in art and urban design. The absence of a spiritual atmosphere breeds professionals who lack reflection and innovation.

A Muslim relates to the Quran in an organic and lively way that influences his/her visual and intellectual abilities and intelligences. This relationship characterizes the identity of Islamic art in terms of harmony, repetition, multiplicity, regularity and variety. Islamic spirituality is related to Islamic art. Through the five daily prayers, reading the Quran and repeating certain prayers as a form of remembrance (*dhikr*), the soul of the Muslim is remoulded into a mosaic of spiritual attitudes that emphasize the grandeur of God.

The Quran says, "Nothing is greater than the Remembrance of God", and this can be attained through meditation and reflection on the creation of humans, the cosmos and the natural environment. Thus, art appears to transform the physical environment into a reflection of the spiritual world. The key mission of the artist is to translate Islamic values into an aesthetic language of patterns and designs that are reflected in urban design and the built environment. Hence, the objective of Islamic art is to enhance the naturalistic intelligence and human consciousness of the Creator.

10. *Unity of the physical and the spiritual:* Aesthetically, Islamic art and architecture represent the spiritual and physical aspects of the lives of Muslims which revolve around the concept of *tawhid* as discussed by Al- Faruqi (1998). The geometrical shapes, centred on a circle or axis, all convey spiritual and physical meanings with respect to the cosmos and human life. The central reference of God in the Universe and the spiritual world is followed by the central location of the *Ka'ba* and Mecca City on earth. Thus, the spiritual and temporal life of Muslims is regulated in circles which revolve around an axis and represent the constant revolving movement of the believer's life towards a human journey for the conscious evolution of God and human destiny. This is also manifested in the pilgrimage and moving around the *Ka'ba* (*tawaf*).

The following section addresses the conditions and the state of the collapse of innovative cities.

7.4 The collapse of innovative cities

Disruptive innovation in cities may occur after natural disasters like the fires in Chicago in the nineteenth century or after human-made wars and armed conflicts as the cases of Beirut in the 1970s and the on-going conflicts in Yemen, Baghdad, Libya and Syria. The reconstruction and rebuilding of cities is a creative process that requires an integral innovation at all levels and domains.

The collapse of nations and cities is attributed to a number of reasons including the inability to adapt and change, the lack of an enabling environment for harnessing technology and talent, or the lack of a culture of reconciliation and tolerance. The key cities in the MENA region (Damascus, Baghdad, Cairo and Jerusalem) are currently experiencing a state of entropy and disorder. The conditions and reasons for the collapse of these cities are outlined below:

- A lack of economic and political innovation and social cohesion;

- An absence of transformational leadership and global vision;

- A harnessing of ICT technology for social networking and protest;

- A lack of social equity and a culture for tolerance and reconciliation.

The situation in key historical MENA cities required a critical review after the transition that took place during and after the period of 2011–2015 in the region as the result of the Arab Spring. In essence, five core reasons were identified as the root causes for the collapse of Arab cities which prompted regime change and on-going deep conflict as documented by Alissa (2012):

1. *Economic model of development*: The adoption of improper economic policies led to a widening of the gap between the rich and poor and a rise in the number of alienated youth. After five decades of independence, the political centralized regimes failed to meet the basic demands and aspirations of the public. Rentier states could not cope with the growing demands of the young. Privatization policies in Tunisia and Egypt failed to provide sufficient social benefits for the poor. For example, the IMF recipe for Tunisia before 2011 was as follows:

   a. Subsidy to remain at a lower level than 2009 despite an increase in commodity prices in the international market;

   b. Deficit to be financed through domestic resources;

   c. New loans to cover the repayment of external debts.

   In addition, the social contract and social welfare state model were not able to offer enough resources and jobs for the growing youth population. This poor economic and social situation led to an incendiary event involving a street vendor in Tunisia who lost hope of a decent life and burned himself as a sign of the psychological rupture between the masses and the rulers. The public space in the city was the theatre for protest and demonstrations to highlight the state of injustice and demands for freedom and dignity.

2. *Political instability*: Economic liberalization without political reform is a recipe for social unrest. The basic demands in the city streets in Tunisia, Egypt, Yemen, Libya and Syria were simply centred on freedom, human dignity and social justice. Centres of power led by the military, secular parties and tribes constrained windows of opportunity for reform and social equity. This resulted in a state of political stagnation and the decay of transparent and accountable institutions. A duality of options was stressed by regimes in order to maintain the status quo: dictatorship or violence.

3. *Demographic dimension*: The population of the Arab region tripled during 1970–2010 to amount to about 360 million. 30 per cent of the population were youths aged between 20 and 35. The 2009 Arab Human Development report highlighted the imperative for states to address both human and national security. In 2010, the Stockholm International Peace Research Institute documented that the MENA region spent about $118 billion in military expenditure while the unemployment rate ranged from 16 to 46 per cent and about 34 million people lived below the poverty line (2 dollars a day).

4. *Technological innovation and social media*: Globalization and social media played an instrumental role in placing the protests of the masses in the global arena. The youth became sensitive to universal values of human rights and freedom. They mastered the art of virtual communication and showed models of social innovation that influenced public opinion and public policy. The street occupants represented the legitimate voice of freedom and dignity.

5. *The role of education*: The withdrawal of the state from the public education sector led to the emergence of the private-for-profit sector which in turn eroded social cohesion, weakened national identity and formed sub-cultures.

In sum, the multiplier effect of inadequate public economic and social policies, political stagnation and technological innovations in ICT had led to a watershed. However, one key lesson we have learned from ecology is that a stage of destruction is followed by innovative reconstruction. As a rainforest renews itself after fire, cities are charged with immense energy, resilience and vitality after a stage of destruction. Integral innovation can be harnessed to shape a new prosperous future.

7.5 The reconstruction of innovative cities: Mecca City as a model

The following section discusses the process for rebuilding an innovative city and presents a model of the Islamic city which is inspired by Mecca City. Mecca is a manifestation of a global forum of a green and good city (a *tayebah* city) and is a vivid model for human healing, renewal and emancipation.

The Arab Spring in 2011 revealed the depth and breadth of the vulnerability of Arab cities. This was attributed to poor governance, poverty, unemployment, injustice and lack of sustainable institutions. A reconstruction of an innovative city entails not only a rebuilding of physical structures but also an articulation of a compelling vision for innovative organizations and a sound NIS. The following is a vision for reviving Mecca as an innovative and smart city that is informed by culture and technology.

MECCA AS A MODEL OF A TAYEBAH CITY

> *I swear by the city, and you yourself are a resident of this city, by the begetter and all whom he begot: We created man to try him with affliction.*
>
> (Qur'an: Sura 90: 1 – The City)

The term "Mecca", which was mentioned in the Quran in the above verse, has been used to mean a preferred destination (*qibla*) and an attraction point not only in Arabic but also in other Western languages. This generic term refers to a focal point for people to attain value and benefits (*manafei*) in a broader sense in all aspects of life from medicine, education, business, art, innovation, science and enlightenment. The key question is how we can view and transform Mecca as a universal model for an innovative, green, and smart urban space for spirituality, enlightenment and transformation. The story of Malcolm X and his journey to Mecca tells of the experience of his mindset and worldview about the equality between all races changing. In the twenty-first century, in a world plagued with poverty, financial crises, HIV, climate change, pollution and scarcity of food, water and energy, branding Mecca as a global forum for transformation, dialogue, peace and celebrating unity within diversity becomes a mission of transformational human leadership (Al-Jayyousi, 2016).

It is illuminating to see that Mecca City was a source of enlightenment on a volatile issue like race for Malcolm X, a US leader, in the civil rights movement in the sixties. In the twenty-first century, Mecca City as a manifestation of Islamic world views, can play a new role in promoting dialogue and understanding of global commons and inspiring new thinking on pressing global challenges like global finance, poverty, HIV-AIDS, multi-culturalism, human security, combating terrorism, governance and human prosperity. Mecca can and should be the place for reflection and crafting new solutions for the current financial issues by instituting a global *waqf* or Green Earth Endowment Fund to ensure that the current economic model considers ecosystem services and the needs of the poor as part of new metrics for human development and progress of societies (Al-Jayyousi, 2016).

Historically, the built environment and urban centres were informed and inspired by specific concepts and notions. For example, Greece was a city that reflected intellect, morality and ethics, while Rome was about order and beauty, and Jerusalem was about multi-culturalism and empowering the weak and the voiceless. The key question is how Mecca can be a model that embodies a good life (*hayat tayebah*) in all domains of life from technology, spirituality, human rights, peace and governance to social equity, human wellbeing and sustainable livelihood. To put it simply, how can we envision Mecca as a model and an embodiment of sustainable innovation and *hayat tayebah*? This section is an attempt to harness the genuine meaning of Mecca as a venue to host and convene a global humanitarian forum. In addition, it is an attempt to revisit the underlying value and meaning of the *Hajj* which is, in essence, an emancipation journey for nurturing self-mastery, renewal and new consciousness. It will be illuminating to consider Mecca as a city that unifies all three global fora (economic, social and environmental) and commence a new narrative of a city that embodies the unity of a good life and sustainable and integral innovation.

In this section, I will shed some light on the key dimensions of the added value and meaning of Mecca as a model for an eco-city which embodies *hayat tayebah* and a social construction of innovation (*imaratu al-ard*). These dimensions are: a) Mecca as a global forum (*qibla*); b) Mecca with multiple benefits (*manafie*); c) Mecca as a green and smart city; and d) Mecca as a model of the good life.

MECCA AS A GLOBAL FORUM

Mecca is blessed by the prayer of Prophet Abraham (peace be upon him) in which he asked that people's hearts long to visit Mecca for both spiritual renewal and transformation. There is an opportunity to brand and harness Mecca as a global city for dialogue by hosting before the *Hajj* in Jeddah a global forum to address humanity's pressing challenges in governance, democracy, human rights, finance, human health, women's rights, learning and innovation. The essence of pilgrimage, apart from the spiritual dimension, is to share wisdom and best practices and to address the current risks, threats and challenges worldwide. The same can be said about Jerusalem, as a city within which Prophet Mohammed (peace be upon him) led all prophets in a prayer at the Al-Aqsa Mosque, demonstrating, from an Islamic worldview, that Islam is not a new religion but a continuum for all monotheistic religions.

MECCA WITH MULTIPLE BENEFITS

The notion of benefits *(manafei)*, as stated in the context of Prophet Abraham's prayer (peace be upon him), is a generic term that encompasses human wellbeing, livelihood, socio-economic development and human-centred development. Benefits also encompass human dignity and the nurturing of the human mind, soul and wellbeing. Also, living the experience of Mecca should be transformational and a chance to learn from the history and personal journey of Prophet Mohammed (peace be upon him) as he inspired a community to shoulder the human responsibility and to embody a global vision and mandate so as to spread mercy *(rahmah)* to humanity.

Realizing the global challenges from climate change, waste, species extinction, pollution, overconsumption, biodiversity loss and poverty, Mecca can be the global space for sustainable innovation. It can be a living lab to test cultural and social innovations like protected areas *(hima)* and trust funds *(waqf)*.

A compelling vision for Mecca City entails having green neighbourhoods, infrastructure and open learning spaces for reflection and social learning. This implies a harmonious relationship between society, the economy and ecology to optimize utilization of land and natural resources and minimize waste. Moreover, this model city will incorporate a set of eco-innovative solutions in construction materials, agriculture, water and energy use.

An example of an innovative and green city is Masdar City in Abu Dhabi, UAE. Masdar City is a low-carbon city that combines R&D, green construction and transport and harnesses ICT to conserve water and energy. Masdar City hosts an education space, R&D centres and green technology applications. An innovative city is characterized by the following green attributes:

- ICT harnessed to control and monitor water, energy, agriculture and landscaping resource use;

- Green sustainable solutions used to promote green building and construction and conserve water and energy use;

- Enabled R&D and innovations to support green technology solutions and applications for efficient resource usage and waste management.

The development of an innovative eco-city entails a range of technological, processes and products along with open and eco-innovations. There is evidence that a transition to innovative cities is a key for competitiveness. Several policy instruments can promote sustainability-oriented innovation in cities like green taxes and eco-labelling.

In sum, rebuilding new innovative cities in the MENA region in countries like Syria, Egypt, Yemen, Iraq, Palestine and Libya requires an integral innovation system to transform society, the economy and ecology. This entails a social construction of technology, new business models and an enabling environment for open and user innovation.

References and related bibliography

Afsaruddin, A. (2005). *The Philosophy of Islamic Education: Classical Views and M. Fethullah Gülen's Perspectives*. Presented at the conference Islam in the Contemporary World: The Fethullah Gülen Movement in Thought and Practice, organized by the Boniuk Center for the Study and Advancement of Religious Tolerance at Rice University, Houston, pp. 12–13.

Al-Faruqi, I. R. (1998). *Islam and Other Faiths*. Herndon, VA: IIIT.

Alissa, R. I. (2012). Building for Oil: Corporate Colonialism, Nationalism and Urban Modernity in Ahmadi, 1946–1992. PhD dissertation, University of California, Berkeley.

Al-Jayyousi, O. R. (2016). *Islam and Sustainable Development: New Worldviews*. Abingdon: Routledge.

Capra, F. (1996). *The Web of Life: A New Scientific Understanding of Living Systems*. New York: Anchor Books.

Florida, R. (2002). *The Rise of the Creative Class and how It's Transforming Work, Leisure, Community and Everyday Life*. New York: Basic Books.

Florida, R. (2005). Cities and the creative class. In: Lin, J. and Mele, C. (eds). *The Urban Sociology Reader*. Oxon: Routledge, pp. 290–301.

Florida, R. (2008): *Who's Your City? How the Creative Economy is Making Where to Live the Most Important Decision of Your Life*. New York: Basic Books.

Hahn, J. (2010). Creative Cities and (Un)Sustainability–Cultural Perspectives. *Cultura21 eBooks Series on Culture and Sustainability, 3*.

Harvey, D. (1985). *The Urbanization of Capital: Studies in the History and Theory of Capitalist Urbanism*. Oxford: Basil Blackwell.

Hawken, P., Lovins, A. B., and Lovins, L. H. (1999). *Natural Capitalism: The Next Industrial Revolution*. London: Earthscan.

Hawkes, J. (2003). *The Fourth Pillar of Sustainability. Culture's Essential Role on Public Planning*. Victoria: Cultural Development Network.

Klein, N. (2008). *The Shock Doctrine: The Rise of Disaster Capitalism*. London: Penguin.

Landry, C. (2008). The creative city: its origins and futures. *Urban Design*, New Series, 106, 14.

Landry, C. (2012). *The Creative City: A Toolkit for Urban Innovators*. London: Earthscan.

Peck, J. (2005). Struggling with the Creative Class. *International Journal of Urban and Regional Research*, 29(4), 740–770.

Reckwitz, A. (2002). The status of the "material" in theories of culture: from "social structure" to "artefacts". *Journal for the Theory of Social Behaviour*, 32(2), 195–217.

Sassen, S. (1994): *Cities in a World Economy*. Thousand Oaks, CA: Pine Forge Press.

8

Organizational innovation

The AGU in Bahrain is an example of regional integration that is characterized by balance between local identity and global integrity, excellence in innovation, and a focused research agenda to address GCC priorities.

(The author)

8.1 Overview

This chapter addresses the third component of the ICON enablers for the integral innovation model. Having considered *individual* and *community* innovation, *organizational* innovation represents the context and operation field for innovation. Ensuring continuity and confluence between the individual, community/city and organization is key to developing a sustainable and resilient organization. Innovation must be embedded and mainstreamed in the organizational culture including its technology, products, processes and paradigms. This chapter will highlight a theoretical background and will conclude with a case study on organizational innovation.

8.2 Introduction

Innovations are framed by institutional context, technology and culture. However, in many developing countries there is a disconnect between the four pillars of innovation, i.e. ICON. Moreover, there is another disconnect at the core as manifested in the dislocation of culture and ecology from technical and economic innovation due to the linking of modernization to Westernization during the colonial era. These two systemic and structural discontinuities are barriers that limit the propensity and capacity to innovate. High intensity and velocity of the "flow of innovation" across the two domains – ICON and CETE – are vital for a sustainable innovation. Hence, it is necessary to deconstruct the barriers for integral innovation so as to root innovation in the culture and ecology and to enable connectivity of individual innovation to organizational and national domains.

Using the metaphor of Newton's apple, many people who lived in the same era did not notice or even conceptualize the phenomenon of gravity because there were a number of discontinuities between looking and seeing; seeing and analysing; analysing and theorizing. Identifying and unlocking the potential of the individual lies at the heart of integral innovation. The innovative individual is the catalyst and lever for reconnecting the community with the organization and also for embedding the cultural and ecological innovation in the NIS. However, this innovative individual will only flourish if he/she is rooted in the right habitat or ecosystem that nurtures learning, feedback, design and innovation.

Learning organizations are designed to ensure connectivity between individuals and the NIS. Key characteristics of a learning organization include having a shared vision, team learning, system thinking and capacity for knowledge creation. It will be insightful to understand the ecology of the organization and the natural phases which include pioneering, growth to innovation and decay/renewal. Managing innovation in all stages (or in all seasons) is vital for ensuring sustainable innovation.

Innovation may be seen as part of contextual leadership and organizational learning. Hence, instilling systems for continuous improvement, learning and organizational development is essential to the innovation journey (Van de Ven, et al., 1999). Moreover, innovation is an overarching concept that includes the strategic intent, operations, systems, products and processes. As argued by Weicke (1979), an innovative system is characterized as "organizing" since it provides an enabling ecosystem for exploration, imagination, adoption and diffusion of new ideas. The ability of an organization to innovate is a pre-condition for the successful utilization of emerging ideas, people and technologies.

However, technological innovation is likely to open a window of opportunity for organizations to introduce new models of operations, products and systems. The introduction of new technology often presents complex opportunities and challenges for organizations, leading to changes in business models and organizational structure and culture. The proper alignment of human resources, technology and organizational systems is imperative to cultivate the innovative potential of individuals and organizations. Organizational and technological innovations are intertwined but new technology may induce instability and change in organizations. Schumpeter (1950) anticipated the impact of technology on the organizational capacity. He viewed organizational changes and the introduction of new products, processes and markets as driving forces for inducing a state of bounded instability or even a "creative destruction". In addition, organizational innovation entails the adoption of a new culture, paradigm, business model and technology (Daft, 1978; Damanpour and Evan, 1984; Damanpour, 1996). Organizational innovation depends on the structure and governance of organizations since they both influence and determine the propensity of an organization to innovate (Mintzberg, 1979). The combination and internalization of tacit and explicit knowledge determines the capacity of an organization to learn as argued by Nonaka and Takeuchi (Nonaka, 1994; Nonaka and Takeuchi, 1995).

The following sections attempt to address the inter-connections between the various theories (organizational design, organizational learning and organizational change) and innovation.

8.3 Organizational design and innovation

Since organizations are part of complex natural, social and physical systems, predicting the sources and drivers for organizational innovation requires a deep understanding of the relationship between organizational design, environment and organizational performance.

The classical theory of organizational design is based on the idea that there is an optimum single solution to problems in organizations. Later, through practice, there came a realization that every organization should be dealt with as a unique case due to the diversity of organizational structures and operations (Blau, 1970), technology (Perrow, 1970) and environments (Lawrence and Lorsch, 1967). One of the key questions to be addressed is *how organizational structure influences innovation.*

Burns and Stalker (1961) examined the effect of technology on organizational structure and the capacity to innovate. They classified organizations into two main types: mechanistic and organic.

The *mechanistic organization* represents the conventional view of an organization that is systematic and stable and has the following characteristics:

- Tasks are well defined and specific with key performance indicators;

- Communication is formal and centralized;

- Knowledge is confined to limited policy circles;

- Interactions between organizational levels are formalized.

The *organic organization* is more responsive and adaptive to the external environment. Its characteristics are:

- Individuals are a key part of strategic thinking;

- Tasks evolve and individuals are open to emergence and change;

- Knowledge is decentralized across the organization;

- Learning and knowledge management rely on networks and alliances.

Organizational forms are shaped by both strategic intent and strategy. It is insightful to realize that there is a correlation between organizational structure and innovation capacity. It was discovered that a multi-divisional form of an organization is more equipped to respond to dynamic and diverse market changes (Chandler, 1962). In light of the theory of "the innovative enterprise" developed by Lazonick and West (1998), the key concepts are outlined below:

- Corporate strategy and structure define and shape the competitive advantage of the organization which in turn defines the level of organizational innovation;

- Organizational integration is the key to achieving a competitive advantage and accelerates innovation within organizations. This was evident in US companies such as IBM and the electronics and automobiles industry in Japan where they have capacity to integrate shop-floor workers and enterprise networks;

- Incremental innovation is important, but radical innovation is the key to forming an innovative organization;

- The governance structures and organizational culture define the rate and direction of organizational innovation.

Teece (1998) made a distinction between "autonomous" and "systemic" innovation to characterize the context of organizational innovation. An autonomous innovation is one that can be introduced to the market without major changes as in the case of solar energy in housing or roads. In contrast, the adoption and diffusion of solar cars or self-drive Google smart cars will require the complete transformation of urban infrastructure. In sum, analysis suggests that organizations develop collective cognitive and interpretive capacity which affects organizational innovation and knowledge creation.

8.4 Organizational learning and innovation

Innovation can be understood as a process of learning and knowledge creation within an organizational setting. One of the key issues in organizational learning is the question of how organizations translate individual insights into the organizational arena. The following are the key concepts that influence innovations in organizations:

- Team learning is the cornerstone for both individual and organizational learning since learning is contextual;

- Social interaction and collective learning are crucial for organizational learning;

- Communities of practice constitute a key component in knowledge creation and organizational learning.

Nonaka's theory of knowledge creation is based on the notions that tacit knowledge represents the root of human knowledge (Nonaka, 1994; Nonaka and Takeuchi, 1995). In essence, the organization is viewed as the ecosystem where learning and knowledge creation take place.

One of the key features of learning and knowledge creation is that it is cumulative and path-dependent (Prahalad and Hamel, 1990). Moreover, it was found out that organizational learning in technology is cumulative and linked to core competences (Dosi, 1988; Pavitt, 1991). Levinthal and March (1993) argue that organizations are likely to suffer from the "competency trap" (March, 1991) since they focus on their core competencies and do not explore new domains of learning.

Balancing the competing goals of exploitation and exploration is a challenge for sustainable innovation. Empirical research has shown that open and user innovation is a source of innovation in many sectors like information technology, health and sport (von Hippel, 1988; Lundvall, 1992). Sustainable innovation is based on the organizational ability to focus on the core business and at the same time to respond and adapt to the external environment and cope with a state of creative destruction (Teece and Pisano, 1994).

Several forms of organizations have evolved to respond to radical technological innovations and global change in a knowledge-based economy. These include: "lean production" (Womack, Jones and Roos, 1990), "hypertext organization" (Nonaka and Takeuchi, 1995), "cellular forms" (Miles, et al., 1997); "modular forms" (Galunic and Eisenhardt, 2001) and "project-based networks" (DeFillippi, 2002). Moreover, research institutions and R&D centres form virtual research groups and alliances to deliver quality higher education, as illustrated in Case Study 8.1 in this chapter.

In addition, flash or *ad hoc* organizations are formed to conduct tasks or projects by specialized teams. This form of organizations is adequate to address emerging and complex problems since it is flexible and adaptive. The sustainability of these *ad hoc* organizations is underpinned by the existence of adaptive and talented teams and communities of practice as in the case of technology firms in Silicon Valley (Bahrami and Evans, 2000; Angels, 2000). A radical type of this *ad hoc* project-based form of organization is known as a "spaghetti organization", as presented by Foss (2003).

The modes and patterns of innovation and technological change vary based on the institutional frameworks and market mechanisms. It is evident that coordinated market economies such as Japan and Germany have a tendency for supporting incremental innovation. On the other hand, liberal market economies are more likely to promote *ad hoc* organizations which have capacity to embody a model of radical innovation. In addition, service organizations like universities and financial institutions provide an enabling environment for organizational innovation (Lam, 2000; Casper, 2000).

In sum, to ensure sustainable innovation in organizations, it is imperative to enhance a climate for shared and collective team learning through communication and cross-fertilization of ideas within communities of practice.

8.5 Organizational change and innovation

The ecology of organizations can be informed by ecological science in which evolutionary changes follow selection processes and the "survival of the fittest" concept applies in the dynamics of succession and renewal. However, understanding how organizations manage change is one of the key challenges in management and organizational theory (Lewin and Volberda, 1999). Three domains of knowledge are applied to understanding organizational change. These include institutional and evolutionary theories and strategic adaptation. The evolutionary theories view organizations as organic systems which are in a stable equilibrium but pass through incremental changes and may adapt to radical changes due to technological innovations. On the other hand, strategic adaptation views organizations as interactive and responsive to the external environment with the capacity to learn and influence the direction of the organization.

Organization ecologists argue that institutional inertia and organizational routines limit the capacity of a firm to respond to change. Hence, organizational renewal or succession takes place which is manifested in the rise of new organizations to replace the old ones. However, Nelson and Winter (1982) argue that organizations normally have limited capacity to adapt once they develop core competencies, procedures and routines.

With globalization and new platforms of ICT, new firms usually displace the ones that cannot adapt and respond to change. These new innovative and adaptive firms like SMEs or start-ups are likely to take a leading role in radical innovations. However, the level of success of new emerging firms is associated with the extent technological innovations destroy existing core competencies of the current firms. This is analogous to the basic notion of the survival of the fittest ecological principle (Henderson and Clark, 1990).

New firms are keen to capitalize on emerging opportunities that are generated due to radical innovation. These firms are enabled by the availability of skilled human capital and venture capital. The creation of new forms of innovative organizations is a trade-off between selection versus adaptation. On the other hand, the *punctuated equilibrium model* argues that organizations can harness the times of entropy or disorder to start radical changes (Gersick, 1991; Romanelli and Tushman, 1994). This era of turbulence is the right time for introducing major changes in organizational strategy, structure and systems, and to power distribution and control systems. Since technology and external environments change over time, innovative organizations must adopt revolutionary adjustments to cope with change and turbulence. Hence, organizations should be able to pursue both incremental and discontinuous changes.

In addition, theories of *strategic organizational adaptation* focus on the role of organizational learning in organizational change (Child, 1972; 1997). In this paradigm of strategic adaptation, it is argued that organizational change is a continuous process that includes dual forces of continuity and change. Burgleman's (1983; 1991) study of the Intel corporation illustrates how the company was transformed from a memory to a microprocessor company by adopting a process of renewal that was based on continuity and change, coupled with organizational adaptation and innovation.

In sum, there is no consensus on a common conceptual framework for understanding organizational innovation due to the complexity of organizational development. Evolutionary theorists look at the relationship between innovation and organizational evolution at the industry level using historical data, while organizational thinkers examine the process of adaptation at the level of individual organizations. Innovative organizations, like universities or governments, have to combine both incremental and radical innovation and balance processes of continuity and change to be relevant and create value in a competitive market.

The following case study considers collaborative research alliances in the MENA and GCC region.

8.6 CASE STUDY 8.1: REGIONAL ALLIANCES IN STI IN THE ARAB WORLD

In a globalized market economy, STI provides new possibilities to form collaborative research alliances in the MENA and GCC. Connecting the R&D entities on joint initiatives that address national priorities is key for rooting technological innovation. The infrastructure for R&D exists in the Arab region but there is a need for a shared regional vision and innovation policy. Examples of this include the KACST, the KISR, the RSS and El Hassan Science City in Jordan, the Masdar Institute and the Qatar Foundation. In addition, the KACST, in Saudi Arabia, provides an impressive integrated model for STI ecosystems with a sound funding model that aims to translate R&D outputs into patents, products and services (www.kacst.sa).

The KACST and KAUST R&D agendas include advanced research in emerging technologies ranging from water and energy technology to space and aeronautics technology. Moreover, Qatar initiated a model for technological innovation as reflected in the mandate of the Qatar Foundation (www.qf.org.qa). The Qatar Science and Technology Park mandate is to develop e-health technologies, water desalination, ICT modelling and simulations, and health technology with a focus on diabetes R&D, while in Kuwait the science base was established in 1967 by the KISR (www.edu.kisr).

Collaborative joint research alliances offer an opportunity for open innovation through the sharing of knowledge and innovation networks in the Arab world. The key challenge is how to capitalize on these innovation networks and co-create clusters for innovation and a joint R&D agenda for sustainable development.

Source: ESCWA, United Nations (2015). Role of technology in sustainable development in the Arab region. Lebanon, Beirut.
Available online at http://css.escwa.org.lb/SDPD/3572/5-Technology.pdf
[Accessed 15 October 2015].

References and related bibliography

Angels, D. P. (2000). High-technology agglomeration and the labour market: the case of Silicon Valley. In: Martin, K. (ed.) *Understanding Silicon Valley: The Anatomy of an Entrepreneurial Region*. Stanford, CA: Stanford University Press, pp.125–189.

Bahrami, H. and Evans, S. (2000). Flexible recycling and high-technology entrepreneurship, In: Martin, K. (ed.), *Understanding Silicon Valley: The Anatomy of an Entrepreneurial Region*. Stanford, CA: Stanford University Press, pp. 166–189.

Blau, P. M. (1970). A formal theory of differentiation in organizations. *American Sociological Review*, 35(2), 201–218.

Burgleman, R. A. (1983). A model of the interaction of strategic behaviour, corporate context, and the concept of strategy. *Academy of Management Review*, 8(1), 61–70.

Burgleman, R. A. (1991). Intraorganizational ecology of strategy making and organizational adaptation: Theory and research. *Organization Science*, 2(3), 239–262.

Burns, T. and Stalker, G. M. (1961). *The Management of Innovation*. London: Tavistock.

Casper, S. (2000). Institutional adaptiveness, technology policy and the diffusion of new business models: the case of German biotechnology. *Organization Studies*, 21, 887–914.

Chandler, A. D. (1962). *Strategy and Structure: Chapters in the History of the American Industrial Enterprise*. Cambridge, MA: MIT Press.

Child, J. (1972). Organizational structure, environment and performance – the role of strategic choice, *Sociology*, 6(1), 1–22.

Child, J. (1997). Strategic choice in the analysis of action, structure, organizations and environment: retrospect and prospect. *Organization Studies*, 18(1) 43–76.

Child, J. and Smith, C. (1987). The context and process of organizational transformation – Cadbury Limited in its sector. *Journal of Management Studies*, 24, 565–593.

Cohen, W. M. and Levinthal, D. A. (1990). Absorptive capacity: a new perspective on learning and innovation. *Administrative Science Quarterly*, 35, 123–138.

Daft, R. L. (1978). A dual-core model of organizational innovation. *Academy of Management Review*, 21, 193–210.

Daft, R. L. and Weick, K. E. (1984). Toward a model of organizations as interpretation systems. *The Academy of Management Review*, 9(2), 284–295.

Daft, R. L. and Lewin, A. (1993). Where are the theories for new organizational forms? An editorial essay. *Organization Science*, 4(4), i–vi.

Damanpour, F. (1996). Organizational complexity and innovation: developing and testing multiple contingency models. *Management Science*, 42(5), 693–716.

Damanpour, F. and Evan, W. M. (1984). Organizational innovation and performance: the problem of organizational lag'. *Administrative Science Quarterly*, 29, 392–402.

David, F., Ali, A. and Al-Aali, A. (2011). *Strategic Management: Concepts and Cases* (Arab World Edition). Harlow: Pearson.

DeFillipi, R. (2002). Organization models for collaboration in the new economy. *Human Resource Planning*, 25(4), 7–19.

DeFillipi, R. J. and Arthur, M. B. (1996). Boundaryless contexts and careers: a competency-based perspective. In: Arthur, M. B. and Rousseau, D. M. (eds). *The Boundaryless Career: A New Employment Principle for a New Organizational Era*. New York: Oxford University Press, pp. 116–131.

Dosi, G. (1988). Sources, procedures, and microeconomic effects of innovation. *Journal of Economic Literature*, 26, 1120–1171.

Foss, N. J. (2003). Selective intervention and internal hybrids: interpreting and learning from the rise and decline of the Oticon Spaghetti Organization. *Organization Science*, 14(3), 331–349.

Galunic, D. C. and Eisenhardt, K. M. (2001). Architectural innovation and modular corporate forms. *Academy of Management Journal*, 44(6), 1229–1249.

Gersick, C. J. G. (1991). Revolutionary change theories: a multilevel exploration of the punctuated paradigm. *The Academy of Management Review*, 16(1), 10–36.

Glynn, M. A. (1996). Innovative genius: a framework for relating individual and organizational intelligence to innovation. *Academy of Management Review*, 21(4), 1081–1111.

Greenwood, R. and Hinings, C. R. (1996). Understanding radical organizational change: bringing together the old and new institutionalism. *Academy of Management Review*, 21(4), 1022–1054.

Henderson, R. M. and Clark, R. B. (1990). Architectural innovation: the reconfiguration of existing product technologies and the failure of established firms. *Administrative Science Quarterly*, 29, 26–42.

Lam, A. (2000). Tacit knowledge, organizational learning, societal institutions: an integrated framework. *Organization Studies*, 21(3), 487–513.

Lam, A. (2002). Alternative societal models of learning and innovation in the knowledge economy. *International Social Science Journal*, 17(1), 67–82.

Lam, A, (2006). Organizational innovation. In: Fagerberg, J., Mowery, D. C. and Nelson, R. R. (eds). *The Oxford Handbook of Innovation*. New York: Oxford University Press, pp. 115–147.

Lawrence, P. R. and Lorsch, J. W. (1967). Differentiation and integration in complex organizations. *Administrative Science Quarterly*, 12, 1–47.

Lazonick, W. and West, J. (1998). Organizational integration and competitive advantage. In: Dosi, G., Tees, D. J. and Chytry, J. (eds). *Technology, Organization and Competitiveness*. Oxford: Oxford University Press.

Levinthal, D. A. and March, J. G. (1993). The myopia of learning. *Strategic Management Journal*, 14, 95–112.

Lewin, A. Y. and Volberda, H. W. (1999). Prolegomena on coevolution: a framework for research on strategy and new organizational forms. *Organization Science*, 10(5), 519–534.

Lundvall, B–A. (ed.) (1992). *National Systems of Innovation: Towards a Theory of Innovation and Interactive Learning*. London: Pinter.

March, J. G. (1991). Exploration and exploitation in organizational learning. *Organization Science*, 2, 71–87.

Miles, R. E., Snow, C. C., Mathews, J. A., Miles, G. and Coleman Jr., H. J. (1997). Organizing in the knowledge age: anticipating the cellular form. *Academy of Management Executive*, 11(4), 7–20.

Mintzberg, H. (1979). *The Structuring of Organizations: A Synthesis of the Research*. Englewood Cliffs, NJ: Prentice-Hall.

Nelson R. R. and Winter, S. G. (1982). *An Evolutionary Theory of Economic Change*. Cambridge, MA: The Belknap Press, Harvard University Press.

Nonaka, I. (1994). A dynamic theory of organizational knowledge creation. *Organization Science*, 5, 14–37.

Nonaka, I. and Takeuchi, H. (1995). *The Knowledge Creating Company*. New York: Oxford University Press.

Pavitt, K. (1991). Key characteristics of the large innovating firm. *British Journal of Management*, 2, 41–50.

Perrow, C. (1970). *Organizational Analysis*. London: Tavistock.

Pettigrew, A. M. and Fenton, E. M. (eds). (2000). *The Innovating Organization*. London: Sage Publications.

Prahalad, C. K. and Hamel, G. (1990). The core competence of the corporation. *Harvard Business Review*, May/June, 79–91.

Romanelli, E. and Tushman, M. L. (1994). Organizational transformation as punctuated equilibrium: an empirical test. *Academy of Management Journal*, 37(5), 1141–1166.

Schumpeter, J. (1950). The process of creative destruction. In: Schumpeter, J. (ed.). *Capitalism, Socialism and Democracy*, Third Edition, London: Allen and Unwin.

Senge, P. (1990). *The Fifth Discipline: the Art and Practice of the Learning Organization*, New York: Doubleday.

Slappendel, C. (1996). Perspective on innovation in organizations. *Organization Studies*, 17(1), 107–129.

Teece, D. J. (1998). Design issues for innovative firms: bureaucracy, incentives and industrial structure. In: Chandler Jr., A. D., Hagstrom, P. and Solvell, O. (eds). *The Dynamic Firm*, Oxford: Oxford University Press.

Teece, D. and Pisano, G. (1994). The dynamic capabilities of firms: an introduction. *Industrial and Corporate Change*, 3(3), 537–556.

Tidd, J., Bessant, J. and Pavitt, K. (1997). *Managing Innovation*. Chichester: John Wiley & Sons.

Tushman, M. L. and Anderson, P. (1986). Technological discontinuities and organizational environments. *Administrative Science Quarterly*, 31(3), 439–465.

Tushman, M. J. and Nelson, R. R. (1990). Introduction: technology, organizations and innovation. *Administrative Science Quarterly*, 35(1), 1–8.

Tushman, M. L. and O'Reilly, C. A. III (1996). Ambidextrous organizations: managing evolutionary and revolutionary change. *California Management Review*, 38(4), 8–30.

Tushman, M. L. and O'Reilly, C. A. III (1999). Building ambidextrous organizations: forming your own "skunk works". *Health Forum Journal*, 42(2), 20–23.

Tushman, M. L., Newman, W. H. and Romanelli, E. (1986). Convergence and upheaval: managing the unsteady pace of organizational evolution. *California Management Review*, 29(1), 29–44.

Van de Ven, A., Polley, D., Garud, S. and Venkataraman, S. (1999). *The Innovation Journey*. New York: Oxford University Press.

Von Hippel, E. (1988). *The Sources of Innovation*. New York: Oxford University Press.

Walsh, J. P. (1995). Managerial and organizational cognition: notes from a trip down memory lane. *Organization Science*, 6(3), 280–321.

Weick, K. E. (1979). *The Social Psychology of Organizing*, 2nd edition. Reading, MA: Addison-Wesley.

Weick, K. E. (1995). *Sensemaking in Organizations*. Thousand Oaks, CA: Sage.

Weick, K. E. (1996). The role of renewal in organizational learning. *International Journal of Technology Management*, 11(7–8), 738–746.

Womack, J. P., Jones, D. T. and Roos, D. (1990). *The Machine that Changed the World*. New York: Simon and Schuster.

9

National innovation systems

The habitat and culture of innovation are shaped and defined by a national agenda for progress and development. A national innovation system is a roadmap for a sustainable innovation.

(The author)

9.1 Overview

This chapter reviews the national innovation system (NIS) as a higher level of innovation beyond individual and organizational domains. It also captures the various viewpoints on the value of the NIS in terms of economic growth and competitiveness. This type of innovation represents the culmination of all forms and types of innovations presented in this book. Specifically, in order to realize a national innovation, a culture of innovation has to be rooted at the cultural, ecological, technological and economic domains. The fruition of innovation is manifested in embodying innovation at all levels and overcoming the barriers that impede the seamless flow of innovations from cultural and ecological to technological and economic domains.

9.2 Introduction

Throughout the exploration of integral innovation, this book covers different levels and domains of innovations; i.e., ICON. Each domain of innovation is underpinned by a theory which covers all domains of innovation as represented in ICON (shown in Figure 9.1).

An NIS is defined by Edquist and Lundvall as follows: "The national system of innovation is constituted by the institutions and economic structures affecting the rate and direction of technological change in the society" (Edquist and Lundvall, 1993).

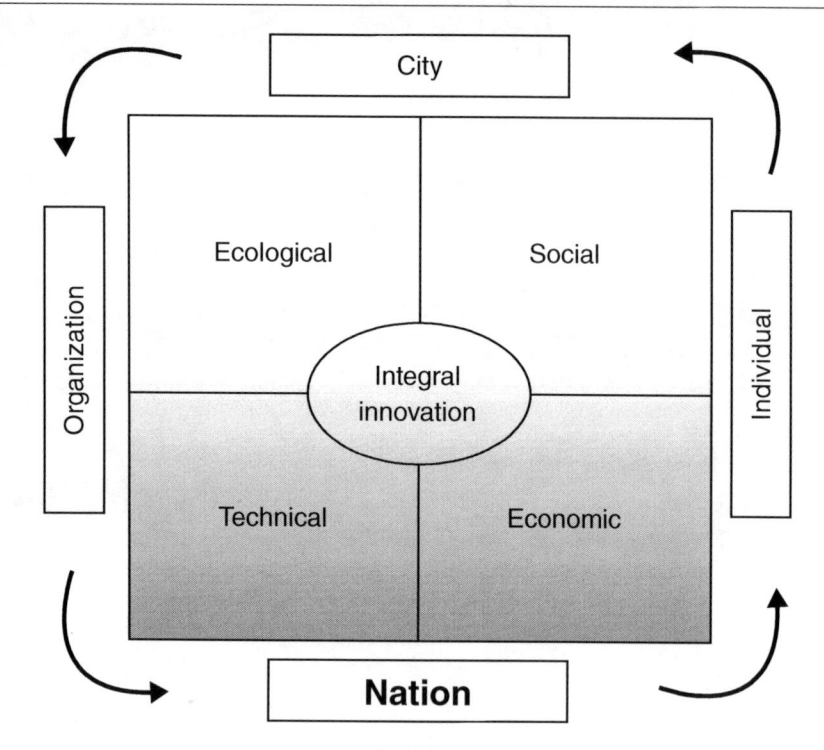

Figure 9.1   A model for integral innovation focusing on national innovation

Innovation is a multi-dimensional concept that entails learning, exploring and doing which contributes to the development of new ideas, products, processes and new forms of organizations (Lundvall, 2000, p. 8). Hence, innovation is not merely an individual act of learning by a firm or entrepreneur, but encompasses a wider domain to include community and nation. Lundvall argues that innovation systems are both social and dynamic (Lundvall, 2000, p. 2); *social* in the sense that they rely on an institutional context, norms and standards (Lundvall, 2000, p. 24) and *dynamic* because they entail the flow of ideas, knowledge and capital across many stakeholders including the public sector, firms and civil society (Niosi, 2002, p. 292).

The value added as a result of innovation at the national level is reflected in productivity and economic growth. Many industrialized countries have a well-structured system of national innovation that includes legal and institutional frameworks for science and technology along with infrastructure and funding models. The imperative to develop an NIS came from the fact that science and technology policies could not explain the outcomes at the national level. Technological innovation is founded on nations' capacity to adopt and apply appropriate technologies and this process does not follow a linear model based on "technology push" or "demand pull" (Mytelka, 2001).

Mainstreaming and adoption of STI requires a deeper understanding of the culture, politics, and economics of STI. Hence, a nation's command of a technology is underpinned by both its physical acquisition and a deep understanding of how and why it works (Dahlman and Nelson, 1995). The key characteristics for an NIS are summarized below:

- It focuses on the networks of people, institutions, regulatory frameworks and policies;

- It views innovation in a broader development sense which is linked to education and R&D policies and is at odds with neoclassical theories of growth;

- Its innovation is linked to interactive learning and not markets;

- It provides a useful insight and tool for policy makers to influence and reform STI policy.

An NIS is underpinned by the absorptive capacity of organizations and individuals. At the macro-economic policy level, technology policy should be designed to enhance competitiveness (Juma, et al., 2001, p. 633). There is a consensus among the policy circles and think-tanks that innovation and technological development are nation-specific and industry-specific phenomena. There is another indicator for national innovation which is called the Systems of Innovation for Development (SID). The SID is different from the NIS in the following attributes:

- Product innovation has more value and significance that process innovation;

- Incremental innovation has more significance than radical innovation;

- Diffusion of innovation has more value than development of new innovations;

- Innovations that are characterized as *low and medium technology* are more appropriate than high-technology systems.

According to the OECD, NIS institutions can be divided into five main categories as shown in Figures 9.2 and 9.3. These include: governments, research councils, private enterprises, universities and other public and private organizations (OECD, 2001).

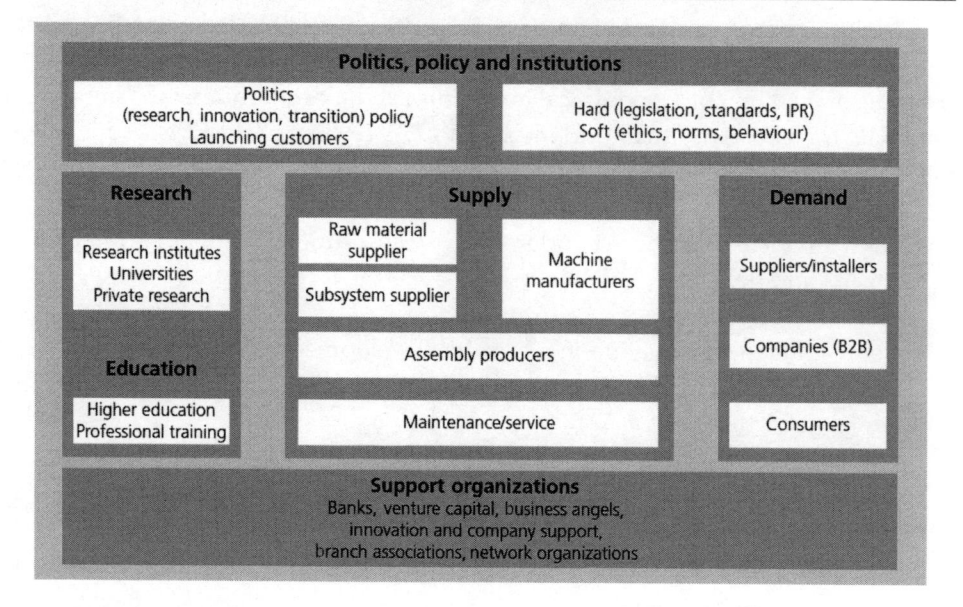

Figure 9.2 A model of NIS Structure (Source: Kuhlmann and Arnold, 2001)

The standard conceptual framework for an NIS is based on a market-led model which is underpinned by technology transfer and adoption coupled with industry-academia collaboration and commercialization of technology, as shown in Figures 9.2 and 9.3.

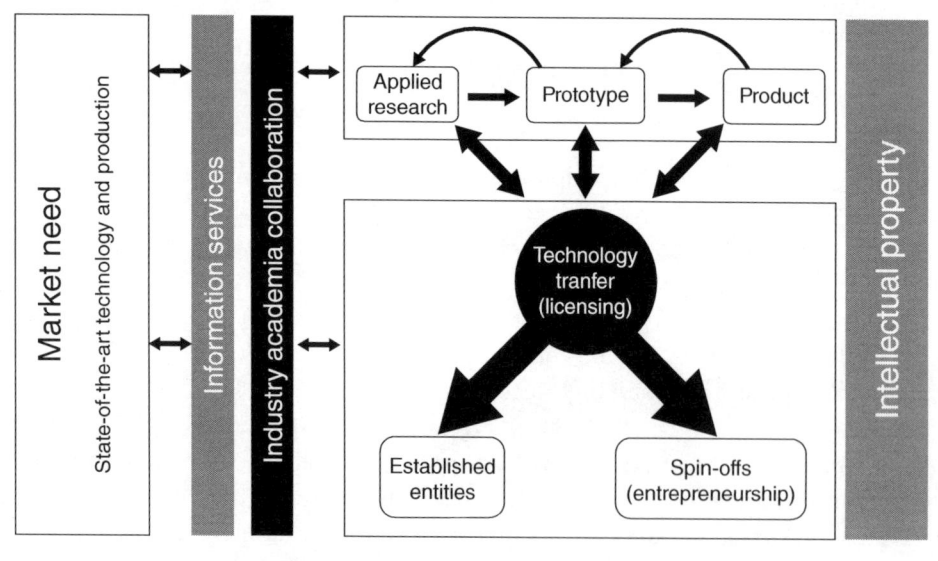

Figure 9.3 A conceptual model for a market-led NIS (Source: Lundvall, 2007)

In sum, the assessment of an NIS entails four levels of analysis: functional, strategic and institutional and actor. The following presents a summary of an NIS in South Korea.

Korea developed sound STI policies which enabled it to transform its economy from an agriculture-based economy to a technology and innovation-led economy. The strategy adopted to build a technology base was founded on the following pillars:

- Promoting the flow of technology through making incentives for foreign direct investment (FDI). The STI policy did not adopt a model of foreign licensing but it used a strategy for establishing key factories, which including within the cement, steel, paper and chemical industries;

- Importing capital goods and keeping constraints on FDI and applying reverse engineering to transfer technology;

- Assimilating technology through R&D, private firms and local use and diffusion of technology;

- Funding and promotion of R&D through economic incentives. During the period from 1970 to 1987 there was a substantial rise in the number of research centres (Kim, Song and Lee, 1993);

- Providing economic incentives to support national firms in the global marketplace. This included tax and tariff exemptions and access to funding (Kim, Song and Lee, 1993);

- Protecting local industries through tax incentives and financing;

- Investing in education and human capital which was clear in the budget allocation where 22 per cent of the budget was allocated for education;

- Supporting the national development plans through research universities.

The NIS represents a holistic approach to innovation which can support the model for integral innovation outlined in this book. Looking at integral innovation and linking it to all components we see the connections between ICON and CETE.

An innovative nation has to align the national agenda for sustainable development with STI policy. The developing world is characterized by the lack of mainstreaming and synergy between organizational innovation and national innovation. This disconnect may explain the states of underdevelopment and low indicators in STI in many nation states. In contrast, industrialized nations with high STI indicators have large domains of synergy between all forms of innovations; i.e., ICON innovation forms. In addition, an innovative nation is able to relate to its culture and ecology to embed and nurture a sustainable innovation model based on local knowledge and human-centred innovation.

In the twenty-first century, building "walls" between nations is not a sustainable or innovative solution to combat potential risks or threats. An innovative solution should be founded on the following principles and code of conduct:

- A new ethical constitution and a unifying social contract founded on equity, merit and justice;

- A celebration of cultural diversity and respect for human dignity and freedom;

- The harnessing of STI for sustainability, peace and global partnerships;

- A transformative education system for sustainable development;

- Good governance for STI institutions;

- Balanced investments in STI for development and job creation.

To embody the culture and mindset of an innovative nation, it is imperative for the MENA region to make a purposeful transition to enlightenment through the adoption of rationalism and pragmatism in science and technology. The MENA region and the GCC should embark on a scientific revolution by reviving the culture and values of the Golden Age. This requires nurturing and rooting of innovation in culture, history, ecology and the social DNA.

The sustainability of the MENA and GCC region is underpinned by founding "innovative regions" to cultivate prosperity and sustainability and to overcome the non-creative destruction in many parts of the world, including within the MENA region. The passion and vision to shape a new future is the core of making a transition to an integral innovation at global, regional and national levels. I like to view integral innovation as a new Marshal Plan for sustainable development. It is simply a vision to transcend the boundaries of markets and governments into ecology, society and culture.

Realizing that the innovation-sustainability nexus underpins the human journey of emancipation, global leaders must be mindful of the fact that refugees play a vital role in reviving human consciousness and the quest for sustainable human civilization.

Nowadays, the world is experiencing deep transitions in global governance, power relations and coalitions. Concerned scientists need to have a voice in shaping the global discourse for innovation for sustainable peace and development. Seeking inspiration from Islamic values is critical to reconciling and to developing a unifying human consciousness and a new discourse for an alliance of civilizations.

It is imperative to rethink and revisit the foundations of STI as a driver for prosperity and development for the MENA and GCC regions. This implies the imperative to root and nurture a culture of innovation to achieve sustainability and prosperity by investing in the ecosystem for innovation.

The following section presents a set of case studies to contextualize the model of integral innovation. The first case study is about innovative eco-tourism in Jordan. The second case study is about Alba, an innovative aluminium manufacturing industry based in Bahrain. The third case study examines Arabian Oud, a fragrance manufacturer and retailer successfully combining heritage, culture and traditions of the Middle East with innovation. The fourth case study presents the Euphrates–Tigris basin as the site of technological innovation.

9.3 CASE STUDY 9.1: INNOVATIVE ECO-TOURISM – THE ROYAL SOCIETY FOR CONSERVATION OF NATURE, JORDAN

The Royal Society for the Conservation of Nature (RSCN; see http://www.rscn.org.jo/) is a model for innovation in eco-tourism and natural conservation. RSCN, established in 1966, had a mandate to manage the network of protected areas in Jordan on behalf of the Ministry of Environment. Hence, the governance structure and the delegation of authority to a national NGO to manage natural reserves is an organizational innovation. In essence, the innovation at RSCN covers many dimensions including the product, process, organization, business model and marketing. It also includes the talent management and the quality of human capital with a passion to conserve nature and develop green jobs.

Innovations in product development were evident in the engagement with the local communities in the Dana Reserve to develop eco-products and souvenirs from silver and natural products from the reserve. In addition, RSCN developed a new business model based on income generation to ensure financial sustainability. RSCN founded a business enterprise called Wild Jordan which aims to bring the products from the protected areas to the urban centre in Amman City. In essence, the rationale was to bring ecology form the rural poor areas to the centre of the city so as to market locally-made eco-products.

Innovation was evident in the process of engaging with the local community, and changing their roles from hunters to rangers who protect the environment. The RSCN succeeded in challenging the mental model that protected areas limit local people's access to resources and jobs. In contrast, the locals are direct beneficiaries from the diverse and wide array of socio-economic projects which include eco-tourism activities like eco-lodges. Fenan Eco-Lodge in the southern part of Jordan is a model for eco-innovation, green practices and appropriate technologies.

Innovation in eco-tourism has high visibility and causes a ripple effect. It transforms the quality of life for local people and enriches the experience and memories of global visitors.

Source: Wild Jordan website. RSCN overview.
Available online at http://www.wildjordan.com/content/rscn-overview
[Accessed 10 January 2016]

9.4 CASE STUDY 9.2: INNOVATIVE ALUMINIUM INDUSTRY – ALBA, BAHRAIN

The Arabian Gulf region underwent major economic development during the early twentieth century. Bahrain is located strategically in the Arabian Gulf region with sound infrastructure and logistic systems. It attracted investment from many industries, including aluminium, plastics, chemicals and food. The GCC region utilizes a large amount of consumer goods. The consumer market grew by 7.9 per cent in a year, with the GCC region spending 221 billion dollars on consumer goods in 2015. Petrochemical industries constitute a high percentage of the industrial sector. The plastics industry amounts to 11 per cent of the total manufacturing industry. Bahrain has high performance indicators in terms of finance, trade, business environment, human development and ICT readiness (EDBD, 2015).

The Kingdom of Bahrain is the smallest country in the Middle East; its area is 770 square meters with a population of 1.2 million. Investors are attracted to Bahrain for many reasons, including the competitive costs of operation, free zone incentives and its being part of the FTA (EDBD, 2015).

Alba is a regional aluminium manufacturing industry based in Bahrain with shareholders from Saudi Arabia and Kuwait. Alba was founded in 1968 and employs 3,000 people. The aluminium sector produces high-quality products and owns one of the largest aluminium smelters. Its sales amounted to 2.185 billion dollars in 2014. It produces more than 900 thousand tons per a year. Other supporting industries for aluminium include Gulf Aluminum Rolling Mill, which is one of the key industries of the East, producing 165,000 tons a year. It also produces aluminium sheets, and high-quality aluminium alloy. Bahrain Aluminum Extrusion produces about 25,000 tons of high-quality products a year. In 2013 Bahrain's aluminium outputs were 1.9 per cent of the total global production; the country was ranked at number ten globally by aluminium output (Alba, 2014). Alba's innovation is linked to its business model since it captures value from a regional market that has a high demand for its products.

Moreover, the firm is innovative in its human resource systems in terms of on-the-job training, succession planning and organizational learning.

Sources: Alba: Annual Report 2014. Embracing the Future for the Long-Term. Available online at http://www.albasmelter.com/IR/Publications/Documents/Annual%20 Reports/AnnualReport2014.pdf [Accessed 15 October 2015]; BEDB. (2015) Manufacturing: Business Friendly Bahrain. Available online at http://www.bahrainedb.com/en/EDBDocuments/ Manufacturing%202015.pdf [Accessed 15 October 2015].

9.5 CASE STUDY 9.3: ARABIAN OUD: CULTURE AND INNOVATION

Trade across continents is an important source of the exchange of ideas and technologies. This is evident in the story of the transfer of the oud plant from India to the Arabian Gulf region about five centuries ago. Trade in the Arabian Gulf flourished due to its unique location connecting it to Asia. However, after the discovery of oil in the 1930s in the region, the national economy shifted to oil-based industries and services like banking, real estate, tourism and petrochemicals.

However, some indigenous industries like Arabian Oud have continued despite global competition in the fragrance industry. The technological innovation involved in transforming the oud plant into a first class fragrance with a local name, Abd Al-Sammad Al-Qurashi, is a success story in product and marketing innovation.

Arabian Oud (www.arabianoud.com) is a leading global business, which started in Saudi Arabia and its niche commodities are fragrance and body care products. It is now a global business with a blend of culture and ecology. Arabian Oud became a global brand with more than 750 stores in 35 countries and more than 400 products, employing more than 3,700. Arabian Oud focuses on quality, luxury and diversity to target high-income consumers, using a creative design and packaging. The key question is what innovative strategies were employed to enable Arabian Oud to survive and continue to grow.

Source: Arabian Oud website. Available online at http://www.arabianoud.com/ [Accessed 12 November 2015].

9.6 CASE STUDY 9.4: TECHNOLOGICAL INNOVATION FOR RIVER BASIN MANAGEMENT – THE CASE OF THE EUPHRATES RIVER

Technology foresight and harnessing information and communication technology for equitable and reasonable water management are key for sustainable development. This case study outlines a basic scenario for the potential of using remote sensing and geo-informatics to build trust between riparian states along river basins.

In an attempt to develop a set of possible scenarios for the Euphrates–Tigris basin, one has to be mindful of the political, social, environmental and economic realities. The context and interplay between these factors inform the outlook for the developed scenario. The uncertainty and complexity of issues that shape the policy for water cooperation need to be taken into account. However, since one cannot capture all these set of factors and forces, only two driving forces were considered – political stability and water governance – in the development of plausible future outcomes or storylines.

Water is only one factor in the regional stability of the Euphrates–Tigris basin. The innovative utilization of technology is likely to lower the probability for conflict and enable a process for knowledge co-creation and learning. Learning communities are characterized by high absorptive capacity for capturing knowledge, avoiding zero sum games and enhancing opportunities for win-win arrangements based on benefit sharing and regional cooperation.

Since 2003, Iraq has undergone major shifts in terms of institutional building and political stability. Both Syria and Iraq are currently in severe states of armed conflict and turbulence which make the prediction of future water uses uncertain. Turkey is emerging as a regional economic and political power and also is an upstream water riparian state. The political uncertainty and conflict have immense ramifications for the likelihood of reaching a joint water cooperation scheme. It is inconceivable to envision an integrated water plan without having an agreement at the policy level on a regional vision for sustainable development of the basin.

In addition, building trust among riparian states can be fostered through utilizing information and communications technology including remote sensing. In sum, necessary conditions for the transformation of the model of cooperation include the following:

1. *Knowledge-based river basin development*: The resilience of the river basin is informed by the accumulated knowledge and wisdom of the past. The value of ecosystem services and the harnessing of local knowledge are critical for establishing a sustainable model for regional cooperation based on transparency and accountability. This will enable a regional river basin commission to make informed and reliable models for water sharing and will also develop an institutional memory and facilitate learning from global experiences in integrated water resources management (IWRM).

2. *Technological innovation*: Harnessing new technologies in water monitoring, remote sensing and geo-informatics plays a pivotal role in developing a reliable water information system for decision making. Technology will support optimum utilization of natural resources, enhancing the efficiency and reliability of water and energy systems. A knowledge-based river basin development will be informed and transformed by technology that will enhance confidence building, transparency and accountability.

3. *Civil society empowerment in IWRM*: The voice of civil society in water and environment is instrumental in building the case for responsible and sustainable development of the basin. An empowered civil society is crucial for supporting sound policy options that respect the environment, society and the economy. Reaching a negotiated agreement that respects both sovereignty and regional commons should be based on a social choice and economic rationality. This will be possible through a deliberate and thorough civil society engagement to build a sense of ownership and awareness of the regional commons and sustainability of the basin.

The key question is whether we can anticipate a social construction of water technology in the case of Euphrates–Tigris basin.

Sources: Altinbilek D. (2004). Development and management of the Euphrates–Tigris basin. International Journal of Water Resources Development, 20(1), 15–33; Fischhendler, I. and Nathan, D. (2016). The Social Construction of Water Security Discourses: Preliminary Evidence and Policy Implications from the Middle East. Cheltenham, UK: Edward Elgar, (pp. 76–90); Kibaroğlu, A. and Scheumann, W. (2013). Evolution of transboundary politics in the Euphrates–Tigris river system: New perspectives and political challenges, Global Governance, 19, 279–305, particularly 289–292.

References and related bibliography

Alba. (2014) *Annual Report 2014. Embracing the Future for the Long-Term.* Available online at http://www.albasmelter.com/IR/Publications/Documents/Annual%20Reports/AnnualReport2014.pdf [Accessed 15 October 2015].

BEDB. (2015) *Manufacturing: Business Friendly Bahrain.* Available online at http://www.bahrainedb.com/en/EDBDocuments/Manufacturing%202015.pdf [Accessed 15 October 2015].

Crossan, M. M. and Apaydin, M. (2010). A multi-dimensional framework of organizational innovation: A systematic review of the literature. *Journal of Management Studies*, 47(6), 1154–1191.

David, F., Ali, A. and Al-Aali, A. (2011). *Strategic Management: Concepts and Cases* (Arab World Edition). Harlow: Pearson.

Edquist, C. and Lundvall, B. A. (1993). Comparing the Danish and Swedish system of innovation. In: Nelson, R. R. (ed.). *National Innovation Systems: A Comparative Analysis.* New York: OUP, pp. 265–298.

Juma, C., Fang, K., Honca, D., Huete-Perez, J., Konde, V., Lee, S. H., ... and Singh, S. (2001). Global governance of technology: meeting the needs of developing countries. *International Journal of Technology Management*, 22(7–8), 629–655.

Kim, Y., Song, K. and Lee, J. (1993). Determinants of technological innovation in the small firms of Korea. *R&D Management*, 23(3), 215–226.

Kuhlman, S. and Arnold, E. (2001). *RCN in the Norwegian Research and Innovation System.* Karlsruhe: Fraunhofer ISI.

Lundvall, B. (2000). Understanding the role of education in the learning economy: the contribution of economics. In OECD (ed.), *Knowledge Management in the Learning Society: Education and Skills*, Paris: OECD, pp. 11–35.

Lundvall, B. A. (2007). National innovation system: analytical focusing device and policy learning tool. Sweden: ITPS Swedish Institute for Growth Policy Studies, Working Paper 4, pp. 1–59.

Mytelka, L. (2001). *Promoting Scientific and technological knowledge for Sustainable Development.* In a paper developed for the Third UN Conference on Least Developed Countries, Round Table: Education for All and Sustainable Development in LDCs, May.

Niosi, J. (2002). Regional systems of innovation: Market pull and government push. In: Holbrook, A. and Wolfe, D. (eds), *Knowledge, Clusters and Learning Regions: Economic Development in Canada*, Montreal and Kingston: McGill-Queen's University Press, pp. 39–55.

OECD. (2001). *Innovative Clusters: Drivers of National Innovation System.* OECD. Available online at https://www.nist.gov/sites/default/files/documents/public_affairs/releases/spi-the-plastics-industry-trade-association-attachment.pdf [Accessed 12 July 2016].

Rao, C. P. and Al-Wugayan, A. (2007). Marketing in Kuwait. In: Marinov, M., *Marketing in the Emerging Markets of Islamic Countries* . Basingstoke: Palgrave Macmillan, (pp. 112–131).

Synthesis and epilogue

Integral innovation is a purposeful effort to navigate through different types, forms and phases of innovation (social, ecological, institutional, technological and economic) as shown in Figure 10.1. The interface between culture and innovation is the key to unlocking the human potential in the journey for a sustainable future. The capacity to innovate is underpinned by a nation's ability to embrace openness and celebrate diversity through cross-fertilization and fusion of innovative ideas from all cultures.

Integral innovation is simply the ability to see and utilize the webs of life. The basic notion of *tawheed* in the Islamic worldview involves seeing "systems" not "parts". Integral innovation is an attempt to harness the internet of ideas and the web of cultures to develop innovative nations. In a market economy that views the value of the world of things, we end up losing sight of the value of the world of ideas. Integral innovation is simply about the web of ecosystems and cultures that contribute to integral innovation. In the current market-led economy, humans suffer from blind spots, nature deficit disorder and ecological amnesia; these human deficiencies limit our ability to capture value and inspiration from both ecology and culture. What seems to capture attention in the business books is technical innovation, or product and process innovation, that is detached from, or not well aligned with, institutional and socio-cultural innovation at the macro-level.

Looking at the integral innovation model, depicted in Figure 10.1, we see the connections between all the components of the model.

Cultural innovation is enriched and informed through learning about other cultures and languages. The richness in cultures offers possibilities for interaction, understanding and a fusion of ideas that informs many forms of innovation. In fact, each culture brings new viewpoints and perspectives that may induce non-linear, dynamic, interactive, radical and open innovation models. Adopting new modes of learning and reflection, with reconstruction and reformation of the local knowledge

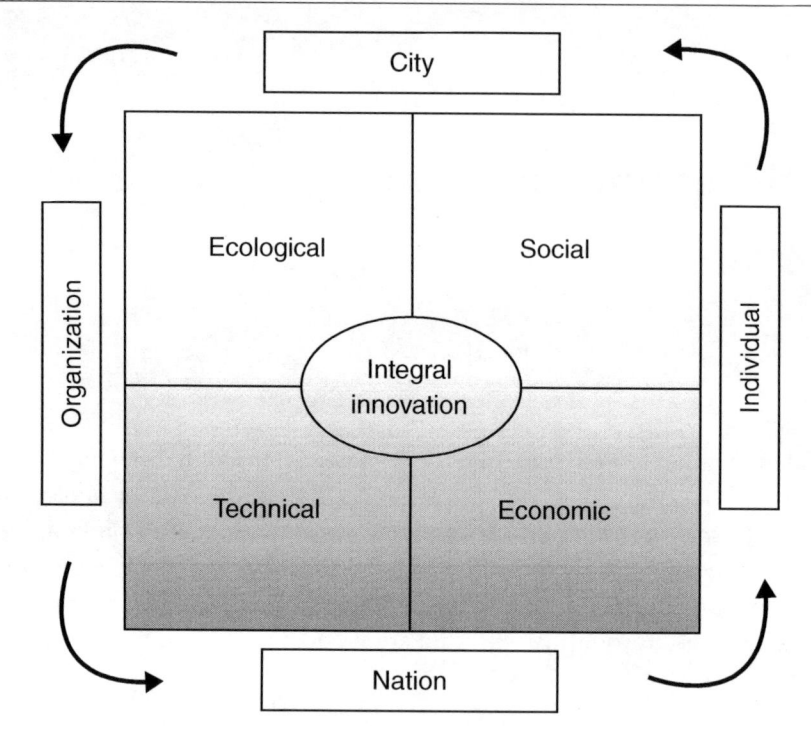

Figure 10.1   A model for integral innovation for sustainability and progress

is critical to making a clear distinction between the two divergent meanings for innovation in the Arabic culture, i.e., deviation (*bed'a*) and innovation (*ijtihad*). This divergent perception of the two meanings of innovation requires deeper exploration to reconstruct a new discourse of innovation.

The notion of *ijtihad* that is inspired from culture and local knowledge constitutes a cornerstone in the Islamic worldview which sees both physical and spiritual knowledge as key ingredients for service innovation, eco-imagination and open and user innovation.

The seeds of hope for nurturing an "innovative mind" come through exploration, inquiry and application of reasoning and dialogue between philosophy and religion. It is imperative to conduct an innovative reading of local knowledge, culture and heritage in light of the globalized market economy, social relativism and commodification of cultures. Social, cultural and open and user innovation can offer new possibilities for addressing core issues related to poverty, governance, human health, resource depletion, financial deficit, refugees and climate change.

An innovative nation can be characterized by many features including having a sound ecosystem of innovation, an innovation policy, entrepreneurship, an education system, ICT infrastructure and SMEs. However, unlocking the potential of man requires a deeper understanding of culture and history. The innovation which occurred throughout the Islamic civilization was a result of the multi-cultural fusion of many nations. It is inspiring to look at the city of Medina as founded by Prophet Mohammad (peace be upon him). The communal innovation model embedded in it was based on the following key components:

- Free thinkers, freedom seekers, believers, innovative individuals;

- A new civil public domain and public space that was founded on an ethical constitution and a unifying social contract;

- Diverse cultures and a community with a shared mission.

This era of enlightenment in the Islamic civilization continued until the thirteenth century and was characterized by universal values and openness to other cultures. Later, this vibrant civilization declined due to many reasons including the fact that Muslim philosophers could not reconcile the two domains of knowledge: revelation and philosophy. In contrast, the renaissance of rationalism in Western civilization was characterized by three elements: 1) the pursuit of mathematical reasoning, 2) the transfer of science to technology, and 3) the development of the institutional setup in organizations. These key enablers of renaissance and rationalism in Western culture permitted a process of innovative renewal and reconstruction.

In essence, instilling a culture of STI in Eastern culture is the cornerstone for harnessing Western science and technology. Enhancing the capacity of innovation requires a purposeful rooting of *ijtihad* in culture, history and ecology. The ingredients for constructing the innovative capacity of nations include the following:

- A value-based society

- Collective responsibility

- Co-existence

- Innovation

- A new consciousness

- Entrepreneurship and social innovation.

At the cultural domain, cultural innovation and the revival of a nation require two components: a *universal vision* and a *historical memory of achievement*. The two parts constitute a combination of the past (historical memory) and future (universal vision). An innovative nation is measured by its capacity to reconcile, adapt and frame a unifying narrative that is inspired from the past and driven by the future. Western civilization has been driven and guided by a number of rational imperatives which included technological rationality nurtured by scientific inquiry and freedom. In essence, the reconstruction of a declined civilization is realized through a process of collective social learning and reflection.

The reconstruction of an innovative nation and culture can be founded on global norms based on human rights, freedom, equity and ethics. For nations in transition, an articulation of both a global vision and a legacy is necessary to establish a new narrative for a global civilization which is informed by a dynamic process of response and challenge.

In today's global crises, which include challenges in human health, poverty, finance, and ecology, the Islamic worldview can offer a fresh and renewed model for a redefinition of the progress of societies. This is attained through the articulation of what constitutes a good life. In sum, rooting a culture of technological innovation and mainstreaming the STI agenda in both national and regional projects are crucial for ensuring a sustainable innovative nation.

Linking innovation to both environment and culture is crucial for socio-technological renewal that is founded on innovative models from ecology like clean production, zero-waste and the circular economy.

At the technological domain, the evolution of technology is an integral part of the progress of society. This progress of technology may be linear but is likely to be discontinued due to innovation or market or policy shifts. In the twenty-first century, the developing world is at the threshold of redefining a new path for prosperity and sustainability that is rooted in integral innovation. This implies that there must be continuity between individual and community innovation and that this must also be integrated with both organizational and national innovation.

In addition, technological innovation should be aligned with, and rooted within, culture and ecology to ensure sustainable innovation. A "blue ocean" strategy seems to be appropriate for the developing world to use to address local priorities and set local agendas. This transformation is imperative to fix the discontinuities in the various domains and levels of innovation as reflected in the integral innovation model. This requires a shift in models for technology transfer so as to root a culture of innovation

At the economic and business model domain, the virtual world and marketplace have induced and formed new platforms and institutions like eBay, Amazon, Uber and Airbnb which require new organizational structures and governance. The intellectual and human capitals are essential for transforming organizations and nations. Leadership and human resources development are crucial for supporting a culture and climate for innovation. The notion of individual innovation is about transforming human creativity into sustained and implementable products, process and systems. Individual innovation is shaped and framed by external factors like education, the market and national policies.

Education plays a pivotal role in rooting a culture of innovation. Transforming an organization into an innovative one requires visionary and transformational leadership. At the community/city level, the transformation of the inner beauty to the outer world at all the domains of ICON is the cornerstone for a transition to a sustainable human civilization. The Islamic worldview is about instilling a deeper sense of beauty, order, harmony and system in the human conscience in order to create a climate and culture of innovation. *Ihsan* is about the continuous improvement of the individual within the community and the awareness of the Divine in every act.

At the organizational level, innovations are framed by the institutional context, ecology and culture. However, in many developing countries there is a disconnect between the four pillars of innovation, ICON, and a disconnect at the core as manifested in the dislocation of culture and ecology from technical and economic innovation due to the linking of modernization to Westernization during the colonial era. These two systemic and structural barriers limit the capacity and propensity to innovate.

An intense and rapid flow of innovation through the ICON and CETE domains is vital for sustainable innovation. Hence, it is necessary to deconstruct the barriers for integral innovation through a process of design thinking and "tunnelling, scaffolding, and bridging" between the broken links in the cycles of innovation in both CETE "the software of innovation" and ICON "the hardware of innovation". Identifying and unlocking the potential of the individual lies at the heart of integral innovation. The innovative individual is the catalyst and lever for reconnecting the community with the organization and, also, for embedding the cultural and ecological innovation in the national system of innovation. However, this innovative individual will only flourish if he/she is rooted in the right habitat or ecosystem that nurtures learning, feedback, design and innovation.

Learning organizations are designed to ensure connectivity between individuals and the NIS. Key characteristics of a learning organization include having a shared vision, team learning, system thinking and a capacity for innovation and knowledge creation. Understanding the ecology of organizations and the natural phases from pioneering, growth to innovation and decay/renewal is important to be able to manage innovation in all stages (or in all seasons) and is vital to ensure sustainable innovation.

The ability of an organization to innovate is a pre-condition for the successful utilization of emerging ideas, people and technologies. However, technological innovations may open a window of opportunity for organizations to introduce new models of operations, products and systems. The introduction of new technology often presents complex opportunities and challenges for organizations, leading to changes in business models and organizational structure and culture. The proper alignment of human resources, technology and organizational systems is crucial in order to cultivate the innovative potential of individuals and organizations.

In sum, the state of entropy, disorder or creative destruction in the socio-technological domain in many parts of the world, including the MENA region, should be fuel for integral innovation at global, regional and national levels. Integral innovation calls for a new Marshal Plan for reconstruction to transcend the boundaries of markets and governments and inform innovation from ecology, society and culture. The innovation journey in this book is framed by the innovation-sustainability nexus. It is also a journey for managing creative destruction, reconstruction and renewal for an innovative nation, government, organization, city and individual. It is a purposeful attempt at the reconstruction of an innovative mind and ICON. This requires a deeper understanding of culture, ecology, technology and the national agenda for sustainable development.

The innovation-sustainability nexus underpins the journey of innovation management in the domains of ideas, individuals, organizations and social structures. Reflecting on the cycles of history and the rise and fall of civilizations, it becomes clear that innovation emerges after a state of deconstruction or an unsteady state in organizations and nations. Refugees play a vital role in innovation but the global consciousness and vision needs to see the ocean of "possibilities" not the swamps of "threats".

The GCC and MENA regions were the cradle of global human civilizations and contributed to enlightenment and scientific discoveries in the Golden Age; this social DNA of innovation should be rooted in the local context to ensure the innovation-sustainability nexus. It would be illuminating to envision new innovative communities/cities in Damascus, Baghdad, Sanaa, Tripoli, Jerusalem, and Gaza after a reconstruction that harnesses STI for the sake of sustainable human civilization.

In an era of deep social and economic transformations, seeking inspiration for Islamic values and civilization is critical to reconcile and develop a unifying human consciousness and a new discourse for an alliance of civilizations which is underpinned by co-existence, human dignity, equity and human emancipation. Following the events of the Arab Spring, which resulted in a state of instability and destruction in the MENA region, it is imperative to rethink and revisit the foundations of STI as a driver for prosperity and development. The essence of innovation in all domains of life should be harnessed to enable individuals, organizations and societies to embody new worldviews for a sustainable human civilization based on adaptation, co-existence, resilience, reconciliation, tolerance, open and collective innovation, and societal renewal. STI for sustainable development should be viewed as a driving force and an overarching theme for the global agenda. The MENA region should be aware of the role of STI in creating and nurturing sustainable nations, societies, organizations and cities through good administration, cooperation and civic intelligence.

Index